Does it seem that no matter what you do, you just can't get caught up?

You want to become more organized – as soon as you have more time?

Do work pressures, family responsibilities, and numerous demands make mincemeat out of your typical day?

Have you tried to manage your time before, and nothing has worked?

This book presents over 1005 strategies and techniques to help manage your time. Whether it's organization problems, dealing with procrastination or perfectionism, harnessing your motivation, getting a jumpstart on a typical day, or simply, looking for some fast time-saving tips, this guide offers quick, easy to read, time managment strategies.

Dr. Mary E. Corcoran, The Time Doctor℠ is a nationally recognized time management and management consultant who consults for major corporations and government agencies. She has worked with hundreds of thousands of individuals with their time challenges, and is a sought-after speaker at Fortune 500 corporations and businesses. Since 1987, she has written *On Time*, a weekly time management column appearing in the business section of *The Kansas City Star*.

Time Management:
For People With No Time

by
Dr. Mary E. Corcoran
The Time Doctor[SM]

WW

WILLIAM WALDRON PUBLISHERS

TIME MANAGEMENT FOR PEOPLE WITH NO TIME

By Dr. Mary E. Corcoran
Copyright 1999
All rights reserved

Book Design by Peter A. Corcoran
Cover Photography by Tim Pott
Printed in the United States of America
First printing: 1999

Publishers Cataloging-in-Publication
(provided by Quality Books, Inc.)

Corcoran, Mary E., 1946-
        Time management for people with no time/Mary
        Ellen Corcoran. --1st ed.
        p. cm.
        Includes index.
        ISBN: 1-893544-18-4
        1. Time management. I. Title
    HD69.T54C67 1999   640'.43
                              QBI98-1744

CONTENTS

Chapter One: The Psychology of Your Time

Self Discipline for the Terminally Disorganized 2

How Bad Habits Are Formed 5

Rewarding Good Behavior 8

Planning Your Long Range Goals 11

Negative Thinking and Time 13

The Top Ten Time Barriers 16

Tracking Vanishing Time 19

Priority Checks. 22

Shuffling Your Priorities. 26

Boosting Your Time Self Confidence. 28

Becoming Time Synchronized 31

Four Time Myths. 34

Chapter Two: Combating the Stress-Time Connection

Time Hassles 38

Finding Time for Yourself 40

Time Desperation Attacks 42

Battling Work Boredom 45

Taking Breaks To Rejuvenate 47

Tie-In to Success 50

Cracking Your Energy Code. 52

Reacting to Time Stimuli 54

Overwork and Time. 56

Beating Work Burnout 59

Juggling Tasks: Multi-Tasking Skills. 62

Sleep Time 64

Chapter Three: Procrastination

Symptoms of Procrastination 68

Procrastination Ploys 71

Instant Procrastination Excuses 74

Battling Procrastination 77

Five Steps to End Procrastination 80

Procrastination and Priorities. 83

Great Escapes to Procrastination 86

Dumping Procrastinated Tasks. 89

Chapter Four: Fast Strategies to Cope with Time

Gaining Four Hours of Time. 94

Using Five Minutes of Time 97

Finding Extra Time 99

Time Pressure. 102

Jumpstarting Your Day. 105

Taking Time for Detail 107

Interruption Time 110

Three Major Time Robbers. 113

Waiting Time 116

Memory Time 119

The 80/20 Principle. 122

Chapter Five: More Time Strategies

Time Detectives 126

Controlling 50% of Your Time. 129

Bureaucrat Time 131

Using Time Logs 134

Getting Down To Work 137

Time Bites 140

Time Habituation 143

Dog Days. 146

Remedial Time Management 149

Time Planning: 60/20 Ratio. 152

Making Time For Innovation. 155

Banking Time. 158

Chapter Six: Coping With Other People: Maximizing Your Time Use

Five Deadly Sins of Time Management. 162

Time Drains. 165

Being Late 168

Time and Job Performance 170

Criticism and Work Performance. 172

Saying No 175

Communicating To Save Time 178

Time for Bosss Day 181

Favor Time. 184

Crisis Time. 186

Managing Your Boss. 189

Fire Fighting Time 192

Chapter Seven: Quick Organization Strategies

The Clean Desk Imperative 196

RX for Your Desk 199

Paper Shuffling 101. 202

Four Rules for Organizing Your Possessions 205

Re-Thinking Your Work Space 208

Time for Clutter. 210

The Paper Glut 212

Time Wasters 214

Finding Filed Information 217

Duplicate Time. 219

Paying for Time Help. 221

Datebook Dementia. 224

Demoralizing Datebooks 227

INDEX 231

Introduction

DO YOU WANT TO BE 20% MORE EFFECTIVE?

Time management experts agree that we can all be 20% more effective and productive every day!

How do we accomplish this? The glib answer is: we need a twenty-fifth hour to the day (or twenty-six, or thirty hours, if you're really behind!). Despite all our technological advances, we're still working with a twenty-four hour day! It's up to each individual to look at their time use, and decide if everyday, they are working as effectively as they can.

Being effective means finding a balance between work and play, having time for interests and hobbies, and having time to maintain your life, your community, and your passions. Maybe you're concerned with the energy issue: having enough of your energy leftover at the end of the day. Perhaps, you're watching your stress levels, and want to maintain your stamina in a stress-filled world.

No matter what your time issues, you're probably interested in fast tips and strategies to help you cope with individual time management challenges.

Start off with Chapter One, which deals with making behavior changes, tracking where your time actually goes, and priority checks. Next, skip around to various chapters:

Chapter Two looks at stress, energy, and overwork, and job burnout.

Chapter Three addresses procrastination. Of course, you'll read this chapter later!

Chapter Four offers you fast strategies to streamline your time: coping with interruptions, detail, using short bits and pieces of time, and planning principles.

Chapter Five gives you some additional strategies to corral time: using time logs, getting motivated to begin work, analyzing your time use.

Chapter Six offers strategies for coping with other people who affect your time. How do you negotiate time use with co-workers, bosses, and crisis-makers? How do you effectively say no to requests?

Chapter Seven outlines some fast organization strategies, like paper management, file retrieval, and desktop management, and date book strategies.

Time is truly a gift—it's there to be savored and enjoyed. Reread the chapters that have meaning for your life; browse through the chapters that motivate you to move ahead and manage your time pressures. Chart out a use of time that gives your life value and meaning—you have the time!

CHAPTER I

The Psychology of Time

Self Discipline
for the Terminally Disorganized

"Discipline is like cabbage," observed the late humorist Bill Vaughn. "You may not want it yourself but it's probably good for someone else to have." In talking about time management, most people will lament their lack of discipline. Others will maintain they know the "how-to's" of managing their time but simply have not disciplined themselves to use those skills in their everyday life.

How does discipline tie in with time management? Most classic time management books are targeted toward highly disciplined people, particularly, those who love lists, and like to follow schedules. If the first thing you do with a list is lose it, then you may not find classic time management techniques particularly helpful. Classic time management strategies usually work best for very organized people who are good with detail, and have better-than-average memories.

What Works for the Terminally Disorganized?

If you are absent-minded, or if your desktop could supply a Scout troop with a paper drive, you probably wonder what technique could possibly help. The answer lies in discipline. No amount of theory or knowledge is helpful unless you put it to use. State-of-the art racquetball equipment may give your closet an athletic air, but it rates zero for health benefits if left on the shelf.

Time management strategies are the same. There must be a tie-in between understanding the strategies and using them.

Discipline is the essential link. We usually think of discipline as something one simply possesses, inherently. But in fact, it's a learned skill. Discipline often carries negative connotations, and usually our gut-level feeling is that it will cause us to lose some measure of freedom. We may even conjure up the image of the extremes of discipline: the robot-like person who lives by such strict schedules and rules, that any resemblance to a human is strictly coincidental. We certainly don't aspire to be like that!

The Three Factors in Discipline

There are three critical factors involved in discipline. First: your belief that a change in your behavior is important. You may drive others crazy with your time management, but until you decide to change, it's all academic.

At this stage, you may need to use your imagination to picture the change. For example, you are on deadline; you've finished projects with breathing room to spare, and you're simply slowing down to a steadier pace. Stretch your imagination to gain a clear and vivid image of yourself performing the new behavior.

The Second Step in Discipline

The second factor in discipline: use an effective change process. We all know crash

> **Making Discipline Work**
>
> 1. You first, need to believe that a change in your behavior will benefit your time.
> 2. Pick an effective change process. Try new techniques slowly.
> 3. Find a way to make new behaviors stick: bribery, reward, or new, and different motivators.

diets don't work, but most of us would love to lose ten pounds, say, by Wednesday, on chocolate bars and grapefruit. Likewise, crash time management programs are doomed to fail because they may extricate you from an emergency, but they don't teach you new behaviors for the long haul. Integrate new techniques slowly, and give them time to work.

The Third Step in Discipline

The third factor in discipline: make the new behaviors stick. Bribe yourself, reward yourself, or pay yourself, but do something to motivate yourself to keep the new behaviors in place.

Discipline is not a mysterious force; it is a learned approach toward behavior. Change experts agree that the best and most lasting way to implement change is gradually, letting the new behaviors become familiar and repetitive. As you collect timesaving ideas, use only one idea a week. It may sound terribly slow, but if you approach each small change seriously, you will have implemented 52 new techniques into your life in the span of one year. Not a bad trade off for someone with no discipline!

How Bad Habits are Formed

Mark Twain once observed that "nothing so needs reforming as other people's habits." It's easy to catalog other's time management missteps: people eat up your time at long meetings; they don't return phone calls; they think deadlines are rough estimates; worse, they're constantly thinking up new ways to waste your time!

As much as we'd like to reform the world, it just isn't possible. We can only focus on our own time habits. Behavioral psychologists, who try to determine how habits are formed, believe that the key is in the repetition of behavior.

After your body has responded the same 25 or 30 times to identical stimuli, a habit is formed. There is little conscious decision-making after that. For example, if you tear into a chocolate bar every day at 3:00 p.m., it will be a tough habit to break and forego your chocolate fix. You will probably get a taste for chocolate if you miss your regular deadline; your concentration may even be broken, and you may be distractible. Your conscious mind would probably never admit that your daily chocolate infusion is such an ingrained habit.

But what about other habits that effect your time management skills? How do you override bad habits? Many behaviorists estimate that you can rid yourself of bad habits in the often prescribed 21 days. (Other performance experts disagree, and estimate 21-40 days of habit-breaking.) Try these strategies to overcome bad habits:

Steps to Overcome Bad Habits: First Strategy

Identify your current bad habits. It's important to determine how you developed these particular habits, and how they are linked into emotional states. For example, do you have a tough time getting started working in the morning? You may have gathered a collection of bad habits into a routine, such as reading the entire morning paper, visiting with co-workers, innumerable coffee refills, and other daily activities that slow down your work progress. Your morning habits may have developed out of boredom, in an attempt to enliven your day.

Pay particular attention to the habits that engage you in tension-abatement rather than goal-directed activities. For example, does your morning routine help you procrastinate, and momentarily put off the daily stress of impending deadlines?

How to Overcome Bad Habits

1. Identify your bad habits.
2. Recognize the stressors that trigger bad habits: stress, criticism, boredom, apathy, or guilt.
3. In order to change, give up your old excuses for your bad behaviors. Try to see the connection of what the old habit does for you psychologically.
4. Visualize yourself performing the new behaviors. Get a clear visual picture in your mind.
5. Practice your new behavior until it becomes an ingrained habit.

Second Strategy

Recognize the stressors that touch off your habits. Triggers may be criticism, anger, boredom, guilt, apathy, or depression. Sometimes, you may need to pay attention to your behaviors for a stretch of days, to try to link feelings with a particular bad habit.

Third Strategy

To begin your behavior change, say farewell to your reason, or excuse for your bad habit. Instead of railing against the fates for a stubborn habit, tell yourself, instead, that because you now understand your habit more clearly, you can begin to change.

Fourth Strategy

Visualize yourself in the new habit patterns. Spend some time savoring how enjoyable the new habit will feel to you. Picture yourself reaping the benefits of your behavior change. Next, try out the behavior in small increments; practice "shaping" your behavior a little closer towards the desired behavior.

Fifth Strategy

Enjoy your new habit; promise to practice it daily. Your goal is to make your new behavior an ingrained habit that benefits your time!

Rewarding Good Behavior

What do you do that's being rewarded? It's a fact of human behavior: you work harder when there's something in it for you. Many of us want to be more effective with our time and may even try new ways to organize our time. Despite these good intentions, the average person wastes about 50% of their time. Furthermore, it's estimated that most wasted time can be attributed to poor habits coupled with lack of discipline.

How do you retrain yourself? Ask yourself, what are your three greatest time-wasters? They may be woefully obvious: the mere eight hours a day spent television-gazing, or your frequent coffee breaks; maybe your time-wasters are more hidden and elusive. Are you over-responding and solving other people's problems? If that's what's required by your major job description, you're right on target. It's not okay, if you become the landfill for everyone's problem. Does perfectionism and procrastination force you to spend the wrong amount of time on a task — either too much or too little? Are you simply trying to do too much?

One manager, overwhelmed with his job, discovered in a time audit, that he was attempting to oversee over 500 separate tasks; little wonder he experienced his time as fragmented and frustrating.

Determining Your Habits

What habits or tendencies cause you to squander time? Do you fail to plan and then suffer when it catches up with you? Do you fail to set time boundaries for others, and they end up structuring your time for you? All of these questions require some unblinking insights as to how your personal habits get in the way of your time use. As the cartoon character Pogo once said, "We have met the enemy, and he is us."

Trying It Out

Choose one particular habit that you think is instrumental in making you less productive. Resolve to replace it with a new habit, or strategy that will give you timesaving value. Practice the new habit diligently for three weeks. Announce it to others, shame yourself into doing it, write yourself contracts, but move yourself, by whatever means, into performing the new behavior.

Reward Time

Next, choose a fitting reward; this will be the incentive to keep up your timesaving behavior. Your reward doesn't have to be spectacular; it simply has to be a reward that is meaningful to you. Pick a favorite magazine, a new tape or record, fresh flowers, a long walk with your dog, but tie the reward to the new habit. Write it

Rewarding Good Behavior

1. Choose one habit that is not productive; replace it with a more effective one.
2. Practice the new habit for three weeks.
3. Choose a reward: a new magazine, tape, or CD, play time, or indulging in a hobby.
4. Use your reward system liberally until your habit is ingrained.

9

down, and use your reward system liberally, until you have the habit ingrained. Your reward then becomes a larger one of more free time, less stress, and the knowledge that you're more productive.

Planning Your Long Range Goals

It's a coveted invitation: on vellum, it declares: "You are cordially invited to begin planning your life. The favor of your reply is respectfully requested." Now this invitation will probably never show up in your mailbox, along with your bills. Are you waiting for an engraved invitation to be planning your future?

If you've had a pet project that you've been wanting to start, but somehow, have never begun it, you know how easy it is to postpone, and forget your new ideas. These are the kind of future projects that may be important to you, but still become delayed. To counteract this, try setting up a Futures Plan, much like a yearly budget.

A Four-Step Plan

There are four steps to a Futures Plan. First, create a Futures Plan that includes all the long range projects you want to achieve or accomplish.

Second, allocate each project a fair amount of time: enough to make steady progress toward meeting your goal by the deadline you assigned to it.

Third, make specific time assignments, so that you know exactly; (a) what dates you will work on each of these projects, (b) what you will try to accomplish on each these dates, and (c) how much time you will spend on each designated date. Fourth, and probably most important, put your Futures Plan into action.

Making It Work

If you mark your budgeted time on your calendar, you will be making your long-range goals more tangible, and realistic, and upping the possibilities that you will follow through. Think of your long-range goals like tennis lessons that you prepay one dark, and dreary winter day. When tennis season arrives, you probably will feel compelled to follow through, because of your paid commitment. Once involved, you will wonder why it took you so long to formalize a long-held goal.

So don't search your mailbox for your invitation to formalize your long-range goals. You need to be the person who turns wishes and daydreams into reality.

Planning Your Long Range Goals

1. Create an Futures Plan that sets out all your long-range projects. (Daydream, fantasize, or collect long-held wishes and dreams.)
2. Set a deadline. Figure out how much time a week you can set toward your goal. (An hour, three hours on a weekend? Write it down.)
3. Make specific time assignments and transfer to your daily calendar.
4. Follow-up by actually working your allotted time on your long-term Goals.

Review weekly to keep on track.

Negative Thinking and Time

At day's end, reflecting back on all you've accomplished, do you say, (A) "I really knocked out a lot of work!" or (B) "Sure, I finished tasks, but it barely makes a dent in all I have to do." Whether you chose the more positive "A" response or the more negative "B" answer illustrates your perception of your time use. Basically, you act the way you think, so your perception of your time usage has a profound impact on your productivity and stress level.

Creating Negative Tension

Every time you negatively monitor your time use and announce to yourself that you're running out of time again today, your body starts reacting as if you're actually in the throes of a tension-filled situation. Your pulse quickens and your fight-or-flight instincts are called into action. You need to assess if you're really in a panic situation, or you're just scaring yourself, as a way of jump-starting yourself into action. Are you using negative and exaggerated thoughts to get your own attention?

The Habit of Negative Thinking

Maybe you've never thought of yourself as a negative thinker; you may simply have developed some bad habits of automatically catastrophizing, over-generalizing, either-or thinking, or other cognitive distortions that affect the way you view your time use.

Cognitive psychologists tell us that the dominant charac-

teristic of negative thoughts is that they're off base and inaccurate. Negative thoughts are a distortion or exaggeration of
the truth. They tend to be automatic, and creep into your
mind unbidden. They're not deductions or the result of logic
thinking; they are more of an unconscious thinking process.

Dispelling Negative Thoughts

Attacking these depleting and negative thought processes takes a three-step process of awareness, addressing negative thoughts and an action plan.

First, to become aware, you begin by counting your negative thoughts. Behavioral psychologists call this a "baseline." Use a plastic grocery store counter, or transfer pennies or paper clips from one pocket to another. Gimmicks force you to think more concretely about

---

Three Ways to Banish Negative Thinking

1. **Awareness** Count your negative thoughts daily. Use paper clips or a grocery counter. To stop them, you need to know how prevalent they are.
2. **Addressing Negative Thinking** Write them down; chances are, they will appear exaggerated and extreme on paper. Use logic and balance to analyze their validity.
3. **Action** Reality test some of your negative thoughts. Are you?
   Catastrophizing?
   Over-generalizing?
   Thinking in either-or-thinking?

Re-program your negative thoughts by replacing them with more productive and realistic ones.

abstract thoughts, and you'll probably discover you have the same thoughts over and over.

Second, to address negative thinking, and to "concretize" vague, negative thoughts, write them down. In the cold, hard reality of a yellow legal tablet, negative thoughts can be stripped away of their judgmental tone and analyzed more realistically. You're looking for balance and logic here.

Third, the phase of taking action is to "reality test" some of your negative mind scenarios. Will you really lose your job if you're late on a project, or will your boss just become cranky? Are you using catastrophizing to scare yourself into performing? Next, try to actively reprogram some of your more negative thoughts about time into more realistic and productive ones. For example, try saying to yourself: "This project may not be perfect, but my job is not threatened. I can do better next time around."

The Top Ten Time Barriers

Quick, name the top ten time wasters! Most people will list interruptions, phone calls and other people as the major culprits in the theft of their time. Seldom will anyone admit that their own shortcomings cause time deficits.

Time management expert, Alex MacKenzie believes that we are slow to recognize human time barriers for what they really are: the principal obstacles to our control of time.

The Eight Categories of Time Barriers

Human time barriers fall into eight categories, according to worldwide research conducted by MacKenzie. These barriers are attempting too much, personal disorganization, inability to say "no," lack of self discipline, procrastination, indecision, leaving tasks unfinished, and socializing.

Environmental Barriers

The other category of time nuisances can be termed "environmental" barriers: the highest-ranked time concerns in the world. They are telephone interruptions, drop-in visitors, meetings, incomplete or delayed information, paperwork or red tape, reading, and under staffing and over staffing. MacKenzie claims that the "environmental" time barriers are the easiest to combat. (Of course, you add, cynically, especially easy for a man who has written seven books on time management!)

Wasting Time

The average manager wastes two hours of time a day;

that's three months of work in a year. It will vary individually as to whether the wasted time is due to human or environmental time barriers. Ninety-five percent of all our actions are the result of habit rather than of conscious thought, states Alex MacKenzie.

Five Strategies for Greater Productivity

Despite time barriers, there are five strategies for greater productivity are:

First, develop a better way. Living with problems makes them familiar; the easiest way to break a bad habit is to replace it with a better one.

> **Five Strategies for Greater Productivity**
>
> 1. Devise a new strategy to cope with a particular habit that slows down your productivity.
> 2. Hit it hard, and make some significant changes in your behavior to uproot the habit.
> 3. Tell everyone about your habit change. It's tougher to go back on a public commitment.
> 4. No exceptions—you're trying to break habits, not re-enforce old behavior.
> 5. Re-inforce the new behavior by rewarding yourself and practicing it daily.

Second, launch the new habit strongly. If you are lukewarm about habit change, you'll lose motivation.

Third, go public. It's more difficult to back out of a commitment if you've told everyone.

Fourth, allow no exceptions. You're trying to break a habit, not re-enforce old behavior.

Fifth, recommit to your new goals every day.

If you are in control of your time, then you are in control of your goals. If you cannot harness the forces of time, then you simply will not be able to self-manage your work, career, and leisure time.

Tracking Vanishing Time

There must be a Bermuda Triangle of Time. Consciously, you know there may not be a geographical area that gobbles up boats and people, but when all other logical explanations fail, it's a nice theory to have. Likewise with time; somewhere, the month of September vanished, as well as the three days before that important project. Gone — without a trace or clue. If time has a way of vanishing for you, it may be time to match your time use against three tests of time.

Time Tracking

Just like a checkbook, you will have no way of knowing where your time is spent unless you record it, or track it in some fashion. Keep an appointment book or calendar and mark up segments of time. Some individuals keep a work journal; just write a few lines every day about projects, decisions, ideas. Next year, it might tell you how long it took to do yearly reports, budgets, or other annual tasks. However you do it, find a way to get some specific, accurate infor-

Three Questions for Time

1. Necessity: Does this activity truly have to be done? Has the activity outlived its usefulness, or is outdated for your current life?
2. Ownership: Is this really your task? Or, should someone else be doing it? Can you delegate, or hand it back?
3. Efficiency: Is there a better, easier, or faster way to do this task?

mation about where your time is actually going. Be honest: if you really spent Friday afternoon on the phone "net working" with former colleagues and doodling, note it, but at least remember to write in code, or keep your work journal off your desktop, out of your boss's perusal.

Three Essential Questions for Time

The three questions for time that apply to more efficient time utilization are first, the question of necessity, second, the question of ownership and thirdly, the question of efficiency. By applying the questions to time challenges in your life, you can streamline tasks and handle them appropriately.

The Question of Necessity

The question of necessity asks you to scrutinize each activity to be sure it is necessary — not just nice, but necessary. Keep in mind, it is common to do things past their usefulness. Think of reports or meetings that no longer serve a purpose, but are still on your calendar.

The Question of Ownership

The question of ownership asks who should perform the task. Is this delegation time, or time to trade or rotate duties? Look particularly for activities that are below your skill level and could be reassigned. Chat with your boss to discuss possible options.

The Question of Efficiency

The third question, the question of efficiency, examines tasks that are remaining. If you're satisfied that you can't make orphans of the tasks, or fob them off on someone unsuspecting, then ask: "Is there a better way?" This will encourage you to find a faster way using better technology, or establish better procedures to handle reoccurring activities.

Priority Checks

No one can really improve on Parkinson's First Law: "Work expands so as to fill the time available." It's acknowledged to be as true as the Law of Gravity. It also neatly explains how we can remain abysmally busy, yet not recollect exactly what we've been doing lately, or exactly what we've accomplished. It may signal that it's time for a priority check.

Taking a Priority Check

A good priority check monitors your time targets. What are you aiming for? What should you be doing that is most critical for the day? What business are we actually in? We're all familiar with the fast-food clerks, who become so busy cleaning the ice-cream machine, they forget to wait on customers. In reality, we don't scream at them: "You're priorities are misaligned, you dunderhead!"

But, we probably fantasize about it. Likewise, we, too, may fall into the same trap of re-arranging our priorities.

Priority Pitfalls

The first and easiest priority trap to fall prey to is concentrating on our lightest tasks — the no-brainers, the fun jobs, the ones that we can cross off our lists with a great flourish. Unfortunately, they may also be low priority tasks. They may eventually solve themselves without intervention, or simply have been a trivial task from the start.

Time management expert Dru Scott, Ph.D., author of *How to Put More Time in Your Life* (Signet, 1980). suggests imagining your day's priorities as a bulls-eye. In the center are your most essential concerns, your highest priority. They have importance, value, and fit in with long and short term goals. The middle ring of the bulls-eye is for "secondary matters". Scott notes that secondary matters are potentially the most dangerous; they are worthwhile, but they won't give you an optimum return on your time investment. The inherent problem with secondary concerns is that they aren't the most important parts of your job or your life, but they take up your time, and keep you busy. They are a good use of your time, but not necessarily, the best use of your time, Scott maintains.

Priority Checks

1. If your time is mysteriously vanishing, you're probably not spending time on high priority items.

2. The most prevalent priority trap is to do your easiest tasks first – not always the best tasks to tackle.

3. Another priority trap is to concentrate on secondary priorities – a good use of your time, but not, necessarily the best use of your time.

4. The last priority trap is trivial items – those tasks that eat up time, but don't add value or meaning to your life.

Again, haul out your priorities: are those irksome secondary concerns one of your higher priorities? Secondary concerns often fall into the maintenance functions: good tasks that need doing, but possibly not today. Certainly, secondary concerns shouldn't crowd out your central or essential concerns.

Trivial Priorities

The last ring of the bulls-eye is for trivial concerns. Name your poison: the small, bothersome tasks that have to be done in order to keep your life rolling. Trivial concerns may also be remnants of earlier needs and wants; they may reflect another time in your life when something was highly important to you, but now those needs are outdated or marginal.

You have to determine your current needs and wants: you may be holding on to a task, obligation, or responsibility because of sentiment. Sentiment, though, will play havoc with your time management. Try to take a more objective look at priorities that simply no longer have resonance for your soul.

Trivial priorities can be delegated, bartered, hired out, or ignored completely. Trivial matters often serve as procrastination radar signals. Are you sharpening all your desk pencils before you write that letter? Are you reading five financial reports before you think about your own report? Are you engaged in trivial pursuits masquerading as high priority tasks? If your time usually vanishes, with little feeling of satisfaction or accomplishment, youre probably squandering too much of your time on trivial priorities.

Only you can answer this question of what constitutes a priority, armed with your objectives and current list of what you want to accomplish over the long run. Keep aiming for the center of your bulls-eye; otherwise, Parkinson's Law predicts you'll be busy — but you may not be productive.

Shuffling Your Priorities

Time management experts agree that you can pick up an extra two hours a day by practicing principles of effective time management. The problem is, most people would prefer an extra twenty hours; two hours just seems like small change. How do we become so time-starved? Social commentators like to point to the complexities of our modern lives. Researchers have even calculated that the average homemaker of today spends more time on household duties than the homemaker of the early 1900s. (Obviously the homemaker of 1903 didn't have to return her kids' videos, chauffeur them everywhere imaginable, or locate their hair mousse.)

Given our complex lives, then, its easy to chronicle all the things that don't get done, and attribute it to "unavoidable procrastination". It's not your fault, after all, you rationalize, merely the price of living in such fast times. The reality is that you're not getting things done for specific reasons. Some tasks have such minimal rewards, and provide minor self-satisfaction. Do you really think cleaning out your garage will heighten your self-esteem, provide scintillating anecdotes and motivate you into tackling bigger and better projects? Chances are, not. You may be able to give up on the guilt that you've been harboring for several months, but garage cleaning may clearly not give you enough satisfaction, so you simply procrastinate and lament that there's not enough hours in the day. Even taking into consideration that you could gain your two promised hours from effective time management, you'd probably tend to squander it on something fun, anyway, and not clean your garage.

You need to establish what management expert Peter Drucker calls "posteriorities", identifying those things that should not be shuffled around on your list but should be removed from it entirely. Otherwise, you continue to carry around the emotional baggage, and as a result, feel less productive, because you're being nagged by conflicting and unrealistic demands on your time. Eliminate the "posteriorities" that lurk about your home posing as priorities. Realize that the tasks that you berate yourself for not accomplishing, may simply be too boring, tedious, or physically laborious, to have much appeal. Eliminate them, trade or barter them off, pay someone to do them, simplify them, but get them off your mind. Don't let attention to posteriorities lull you into thinking you're being productive; busy, yes, productive, no.

Shuffling Your Priorities

1. Make the distinction between being busy and being productive.
2. Assess the payoffs of tasks: you may be procrastinating (and berating yourself unnessessarily) for tasks that "should" be done, but offer minimal reward.
3. What tasks need to be removed permanently from your list? Trade, barter, pay others, buddy up with a friend to get tasks done that are unavoidable.

Boosting Your Time Self-Confidence

In managing your time well, you have to take control of situations, and master and shape them. You have to set goals and cut out activities that squander your time. All of these strategies are intertwined with your level of self-confidence.

Locus of Control

Individuals who manage time well have what psychologists call, an internal locus of control: they are not reactive to every time demand asked of them, but rather they make decisions and plan according to a larger master plan. How do you improve your time with self-confidence?

Improving Your Time Self-Confidence

Focus on your past successes. You diminish your own self-esteem by regurgitating any of your past mistakes. Worse, if you may find yourself dwelling on your weaknesses, rather than building on your strengths.

Next, pinpoint your motivation. If you are not committed to a larger goal for your life, then you will be like a boat without a rudder--drifting and susceptible to being swept away by any time demands. You'll remain busy, but your time won't reap you many rewards because it won't be directed toward a specific goal. Well defined goals allow you to build enthusiasm and passion for your dreams.

Expecting a Positive Outcome

Another way to raise your self-esteem is to expect positive things to happen. Motivational books and tapes are such perennial best sellers because they work to inspire and motivate. Undoubtedly, you'll run into obstacles and roadblocks on the way to your goals; no one said it would be easy! Obstacles can shake your vision and convince you that your plans are feeble and impossible. If your confidence is wobbly, you'll give up. The

> ## Self Confidence and Time:
>
> 1. Focus on past successes; don't dredge up old mistakes.
> 2. Pinpoint your motivation.
> 3. Expect positive things to happen on the way to your goals.
> 4. Don't be afraid of hard work to master your goals.

differentiation between winners and losers is winners don't let the tough times debilitate their self-esteem.

Keeping Your Self-Confidence Nurtured

To keep your self-confidence levels high calls for steady doses of motivation. Share your enthusiasm with others who are interested. If your current work or social milieu doesn't include those individuals, then find them. Link up with professional groups, hobby organizations, church and temple groups. You don't need legions of back-patters, but rather a small circle of supportive individuals who can share your enthusiasm.

Finally, don't be afraid of hard work. Biographies of famous achievers chronicle the tie between hard work and mastery of goals. It's easy to discount high achievers as lucky, but the reality is, high achievers' luck is often underpinned with countless hours of hard work and persistence, coupled with a sustaining belief in themselves.

Raising your self-esteem is inexorably linked to the way you spend your time.

Becoming Time-Synchronized

In 1876 the Seth Thomas Clock Company added a new product: the wind up alarm clock. Waking up has never been the same since. By the end of the nineteenth century, clocks began to dominate every aspect of people's waking lives. In the 1920s, time and efficiency experts began to "clock" workers to time how long tasks took to complete. The time management industry was born; time logs and date-book organizers became the "scientific" way of estimating how productive and efficient workers could become. Is it any wonder that blank spaces in a date-book lure us like Circe? It's no accident that over-scheduling gives us a feeling of productivity, as well as anxiety. How do we move away from clock-dominated thinking?

Gauging Your Time Perception

Try this exercise used at the Dallas Diagnostic Association, in Texas, where they treat "time-sickness." Check the minute hand of your watch, close your eyes, relax, and feel when one minute has elapsed. Researchers found that everyone drastically underestimates the deadline. An "average" minute envisioned by individuals is usually thirty seconds. How can we realistically schedule an entire day, if our perception of time is so warped?

Becoming Aware of Time Synchronization

Time experts have observed that when you are synchronized with real time, you are less inclined to feel the urge to

Becoming Time Synchronized

1. Watch your automatic reactions to time cues.
2. Assess the specific activities that over commit your time.
3. Write yourself a mission statement and include activities that are your critical values.
4. Begin each day by visualizing the high points of your day: the pleasure benchmarks, and the various tasks that beckon you.

over schedule yourself. Time synchronization (sounding suspiciously like a new Olympic category) requires you to become aware of how much you react to external cues. External cues are those nagging "shoulds" and "have-to's" that regulate and over-commit your time. Naturally, you wouldn't tell your bosses that from now on, you're not reacting to extraneous deadlines, report due-dates and other frivolities. Some evils are necessary to retain items like paychecks and benefits. But rather, assess activities that over-commit your schedule. Is it time to take a hiatus from the professional group that dominates off-hours? Can you get some relief from child-chauffeuring and carpools? Has an old hobby become a burden to engage in now? These are the type of time synchronization questions you need to be asking yourself.

Finding Your Time Mission

Write yourself a mission statement. Divide it into categories of family, friends, business; spiritual/and or community. A mission statement should be a clear, concise summary that illustrates what is important to you. Over-scheduling yourself is a fast route to losing a sense of purpose with your time. You need to reconnect with your own priority system.

Envision the start of each new day with the high points of your day. These are the activities that will give meaning, purpose and joy to your life. Notice they are not accomplishments in the traditional sense, but rather, they are a blend of activities that give you a sense of personal satisfaction. Only then can you think about changing your clock-dominated time.

Four Time Myths

As movie maven Sam Goldwyn once said: "Let's have some new cliches." Time management cliches are: "I'll never get organized," or, "I could never learn to (fill in the blank for any time management strategy)," or "I'm afraid I'd get so time efficient, I'd be obnoxious." Another one is "I would spend so much time making lists and getting organized, I wouldn't have time to do anything else." Time management cliches are very pervasive, and often masquerade as Immutable Laws of the Universe.

Debunking the Myths

Let's examine some of the myths. "I'll never get organized" sounds as if organization is a terminal state. Once you're organized, you never have to do it again. Organization is not a static state, but rather a constantly changing one. Organizing your belongings, your paperwork, or even a favorite junk drawer is just an avenue to making your time more effective. For instance, if you've found a system to locate your tax receipts when you need your car plates renewed, that's organization. It does not have to be complex, simply something that saves you time and energy. Try to add one simple organizing aid every week; it could be a red file for current papers, a ream of notepads for the home phone, or a system for expunging old magazines.

Trying New Behaviors

"I could never do that!" Referring of course, to any new

way of approaching time that seems unfamiliar and awkward. Chances are, you couldn't roller skate once, either, but you eventually learned. Often, we feel self-conscious about trying a timesaving technique because it doesn't feel like

Battling Time Myths

1. Try one new organizing tactic per week.
2. Give a new strategy time before you give up on it.
3. The reality is realistically, a little organization will not make you time-obsessed.

our usual behavior. A person who is continually late will, indeed, feel strange, sitting in a waiting room with minutes to spare. Those who write lists on the backs of parking receipts will feel presumptuous making lists on printed To Do sheets. Give a new strategy some time before you discard it. Twist it around, personalize it, give it your own stamp before you attest that it doesn't work for you.

Myth Number Three

Myth number three is that "I'll get so organized, I'll be obnoxious." This is of course, precluding that you weren't previously obnoxious. We fear that time management techniques will make us too regimented and constricted, and for proof, we usually envision the most obsessive and compulsive person we've ever encountered, and thank the gods that we are not yet, that neurotic and driven to save time. We dredge up case studies from the files of the truly time-obsessed: The character who times you with a stop watch, when you ask for a minute of his time, or the individual who files his 4:00 cookie snack in a mani-

la file folder. All sad, but true cases — and vow we will never suc-
cumb to time mania. The reality is that we could probably
change some of our time behavior without becoming certifiable.
People who manage time well are not obsessive, but believe in the
right to structure their own time, and hunt for timesaving strategies that help them achieve that aim.

The Last Time Myth

The fourth myth, "I'll spend so much time getting organized, I won't have time for anything else," again allows you to
overlook all the time you waste being disorganized. Research
indicates that the average executive spends 20% of their time
doing clerical work that could be delegated to someone else.
Furthermore, the average manager uses 20 minutes a day
searching for lost items. Obviously, if you're disorganized, you
still have to take time for search missions, copying machines,
and envelope-licking. To paraphrase Sam Goldwyn, "Let's
have some new cliches about what you do with your time!"

CHAPTER 2

Combating the Stress Time Connection

Time Hassles

What everyday annoyances drive you round the bend? Traffic gridlock, insistent telephones, over-scheduling, or days that never seem to end? Whatever the hassles, research indicates that the stress of minor hassles can cause damage as severe as major traumas if not managed promptly and effectively. USA Today, in 1997, reported the top five hassles of Americans were concerns about office politics, job security, stalled careers, number of work assignments, and amount of red tape.

Stress Hardiness

Obviously, there is no way to eliminate all the odds and ends that frazzle your nerves, but you can build emotional strength for withstanding more traumatic times. Stress experts label this psychological conditioning program as "stress hardiness." One of the best ways to battle stress is to employ attitude adjustments. The key attitude to toughen up your stress reactions is to learn to observe without argument.

Developing Stress Hardiness

1. Observe without argument, or agree with your current reality.
2. Ask yourself; What are my options right now? Be realistic and specific.
3. Brainstorm new solutions. Be creative!

Agreeing With Reality

The next time you're in a traffic jam, how do you react? Do you angrily rail against the fates that created highway construction to personally slow you down? Or, you rationalize that this always happens to you, victimized by unforeseen occurances. Whether you respond in an anger or victim mode, you are still setting up an adversative situation between you and your trauma. A better stress-reducing strategy is to learn to agree with what happens. Agreeing with your current reality means to see it clearly, to accept it, and to problem solve from that perspective. Agreeing with your reality does not require you to be happy with the irritation or problem. You can adopt an accepting attitude toward your stressor, without endorsing it.

Monitoring Your Stress Levels

Instead of arguing with yourself over the setback, monitor your first thoughts when you encounter a stressful event. Ask yourself what is troubling you about the situation. Be realistic and specific: "I can't wait for Sam's late report. I wanted it on time." Then ask yourself "What are my options, or possibilities now?" Again be realistic and specific. Ask yourself the final question: "What if I were to....?" Be creative, and brainstorm about new solutions.

Your New Stress Management Regime

Let's examine your stress progress: your reaction has acknowledged the stressor, but you've observed without argument, and without automatic stress reactions that accelerate your emotions. You've calmed your emotions, and brainstormed solutions that may work. Your success in learning to accept situations of minor importance can lead to building hardiness towards accepting future stresses and disappointments.

Finding Time For Yourself

"I'm so busy, I never have time for myself." How often do you repeat that refrain, or hear it voiced by your friends? It isn't only time that's scarce, but rather the art of time balance, the ability to juggle the priorities of family, self and work. (Even if you're short on family, your "family" could be your community, your pets, or your religious or civic associations.) It doesn't take much to get these priorities out of balance, an emergency here, extra time devoted there, and soon your priorities are off kilter. Time for yourself is usually the first priority to eliminate, and usually the easiest, as well.

Assessing Your Time Needs

Time for yourself is the most unselfish time you can use. You can do more for others when you take care of yourself. When your health is good, when you feel secure, when you're well-rested, and when you're stimulated, you can find the inclination and the insight necessary to help others. To assess your time, get in the habit of asking yourself the question daily, "What do I need?" Is it physical exercise, quiet time to read or meditate, stimulation of friends, interaction with others? Note that this is a different question than "What do I want?" You may "want" to win the lottery, bask in the sun in Pongo Pongo, or other equally pleasant distractions, but they may be also, difficult to implement on a busy Monday morning. Remember the fine distinction between what you "want" and what you "need".

The Benefits of Time for Yourself

Time for yourself, of course, can refresh you, revitalize you, and sharpen your perspective. Time for yourself, in a way that is not fully explicable, can increase your self esteem — your opinion of yourself — perhaps through the subtle suggestion that you are worth doing something for every day. As Winston Churchill said, "We are all worms, but I have decided that I am a glow-worm."

Balance breaks, fun, creativity, and hard work. If you're feeling stalled or stagnant, do something out of the ordinary for yourself. It might be buying a foreign magazine or newspaper, reading a different type of

Finding Time for Yourself

1. Ask yourself daily: What do I need?
2. Get a balance of hard work, breaks, fun, and creativity.
3. What is your single, most compelling priority for work, family, or self?

hobby magazine, doing a crossword, or word puzzle, if that's unlike you, trying a different type of exercise, or eating different foods. What even you choose, get out of your box you've put yourself in.

Keeping Balanced

To keep your life in balance, envision it as a triangle, suggest Richard and Linda Eyre, authors of *LifeBalance* (Ballantine Books, 1987). A triangle has three corners that are equally balanced; there is stability because each corner finds its level independent of the other two, yet supports the other two corners. Work, family, and self are in each corner. The danger lies, observes the Eyres, in not so much in forgetting that all three are important, but in letting other, less important things get ahead of them. Allowing work, family, and personal needs to get out of balance with each other can happen easily. Tilting away from balance happens a little each day, so to get back on balance, you need to set one single priority for each corner, everyday. This takes about five minutes per day to give some thought to the single, most compelling priority of work, family and self.

Time Desperation Attacks

"The reasons that angels can fly," wrote G. K. Chesterton, "Is that they have learned to take themselves lightly." Thinking about time and our deadlines often leaves us feeling panic stricken; to recover from time panic we may actually need to take our time needs more lightly.

There is no feeling so recognizable, and so sinking, as the feeling that you are quickly approaching a deadline, or a finish date, and you have run out of time. These time shortages might be called "time desperation attacks."

Time Desperation Attacks

1. Order tasks in order of importance. Caution: your stress level encourages you to see every task as a priority.
2. Determine why there is an emergency. Is it a real one or a manufactured one? Can you safely postpone, or is is really a high priority?
3. Ask yourself: how can I be most effective this moment?
4. Focus on your desired outcome: what is the clearest, cleanest, more efficient strategy for the task to be completed?

Recognizing Our Symptoms

Time desperation attacks are probably like headaches; they can strike anyone at any time. Symptoms are the frenzied, crazed looks you give co-workers, the sensible realization that you should immediately leave for Nepal, and other divergent ideas that, of course, get in the way of your work production.

First Aid for Time Panic

How do you calm your jangled nerves and become more time efficient? Your first action should be to break the chain of self-destructive behavior; you need to fight off the pressure to do more and more. There simply has to be a finite end to your endless list of things to do: the answer is priority-ordering. Priority-ordering is your only way out of a time desperation morass. Ruthlessly order your tasks in their order of their importance, and attack the list. Ask yourself process questions: can tasks be postponed, delegated, or negotiated?

Simplifying and Eliminating Tasks

Try to get a brief history of the impending emergency. Did your boss just attend a meeting and commit your department to be the trailblazers toward a new management strategy? Based on behavior from the past, will this enthusiasm wane with the coming weeks? Can you safely postpone the task, or is it in your best interests to make it a top priority? Look at other hot priorities with the same critical eye: will postponing them a bit, lessen their priority? Try to be less reactive; don't get caught up in the urgency of the moment.

Your Next Steps: Clarity and Simplicity

If your maneuvering hasn't been successful, and you're still stuck with the task, clarify and simplify. Clarify by asking: how can I best be effective at this moment? What is my best strategy for producing the results I need? Next, simplify by spending some time thinking of the clearest, cleanest route to your desired outcome. What tasks get into the category of nice, but not necessary? Pare down the tasks and get down to the basic, elemental items. Take three deep breaths and banish panic-y thoughts.

Paring Down Your List

Moving out of desperation attacks require classic time management skills: delegation, postponing tasks, eliminating others (tasks, that is) and working smarter, but not necessarily harder. Time desperation attacks occur predictably, when your stress levels and juggling skills are pushed to their limit. Remember priority-ordering and ruthless list-paring are the keys to surviving panic attacks.

Battling Work Boredom

Over one hundred and fifty years ago, Ralph Waldo Emerson observed, "Nothing great can be achieved without enthusiasm." At times it's difficult to maintain an ongoing work enthusiasm. It's not exactly a topic we want to bring up with our superiors. "Gee, this job would bore the dead; I can barely keep awake," are probably not sentiments we want to share with employers who control our future. Workplace boredom affects all strata of job titles, from the assembly line to executive suites, so it's worth your time to do something about it.

Symptoms of Work Boredom

Work boredom is often symptomatic of other issues in your life: a roadmap of your psyche. Some experts believe that boredom is an emotional and psychological signal that tells you you're lacking some form of recognition or fulfillment in your life. Boredom means you need to become more proactive in recharging your energies. You might want to sign up for a new class, seminar, workshop, or educational series that will provide you with new skills or techniques. (It also breaks the tedium of the week). If training dollars are short, negotiate with your superiors to pass on the information you'll gain with your colleagues, either by some type of summary and materials, or by personally preparing an overview. Consider paying for additional education yourself, or join professional organizations that provide stimulating program topics. Offer to serve on company task forces, particularly the ones that bring you into contact with other departments. Try for challenging issues that have an impact on your workplace. Although it might be more fun to plan the holiday office party, you may alleviate your boredom with an issue that gives you a larger sense of accomplishment, past the sugarplum season.

The Pleasure Connection

Schedule "play" time. Be relentless about scheduling pleasurable time for yourself. Dr. Harriet Braiker, a California expert on stress, has noted that when we are bored and stressed, we limit our pleasurable activities, and begin a downward spiral of less and less activity. The same spiral happens at work; boredom zaps our energy, and limits our options to try anything new. When we really need the challenge of doing things a different way, and finding more creative solutions to old problems, we have the energy levels of zucchini. We need to take our "play" seriously, and force ourselves to schedule some playful and fun activities.

Battling Work Boredom

1. Sign up for some motivational training. Negotiate with your employer by offering to share the information with co-workers.
2. Schedule serious time for play. Lack of pleasurable activities and stress go hand in hand.
3. Spend some time looking for the intrinsic value your job holds. Boredom often occurs when our jobs lack direction and personal meaning.

Detecting Your Work Values

Lastly, look at the intrinsic value and rewards of your job. What you do, and provide, does have a consequence to someone, either in your organization, or to customers or the public. You are not performing your job in isolation. It may be difficult when you're bored, but you need to remind yourself of the satisfaction and enjoyment that you gain form the nature of your work, itself; it's a vital element in job fulfillment and the avoidance of boredom. So, suppress that yawn; you have a new task now: alleviating your boredom!

Taking Breaks to Rejuvenate

Thomas Edison supposedly napped on his laboratory tables at odd hours. Winston Churchill credited his daily naps as getting him through the long, arduous days of World War II. Other historical figures have often shared a similar abilities to catnap, or refresh themselves with small pockets of rest.

The Mind Body Interaction

In *The 20 Minute Break*, author Ernest Lawrence Rossi, Ph.D., presents groundbreaking information about mind-body interactions. Scientists, who have studied human performance, have long suspected that the human body functions in discrete cycles of alertness, peak performance, stress, and rest. Now, due to sophisticated physiological monitoring devices, researchers can now measure what before were only clues about mind-body systems. Every 90 to 120 minutes, our body cycles through, what are called, Ulradian Rhythms. Dr. Ernest Rossi points out that after these periods of heightened physical and mental alertness, and operating at our functional best, our brain signals the need for a rest.

Rhythms of Rest and Rejuvenation

"Unfortunately, most of us – seduced by the world's demands and tightly organized schedules – habitually ignore and override the signs that our mind-body systems need to swing inward and heal and revitalize." Rossi's research indicates that humans chronically override this need for days, months, or even years on end. We commonly interrupt our mind-body's natural ultradian rhythms of rejuvenation. The end result is stress, fatigue and psychosomatic problems.

Rossi recommends looking at the "troughs" during your

day: those periods when you are at your lowest ebb, both phys-ically and mentally. Japanese researchers Tsuji and Kobayshi have isolated the "breaking point" of most workers as between 3:00 and 4:00 P.M., and believe that in terms of biological rhythms, this point is the trough of the deepest low of the day's functioning. (For night owls, the lowest ebb may be early in the morning before 10 A.M.)

Scheduling Breaks

For ultimate productivity, Rossi suggests a break every 90 to 120 minutes. It may be hard to explain to your boss that you've spiraling right into the end of an Ultradian Cycle, your verbal and spatial skills are dimming, and you're on the vortex of a recuperative, regenerative phase—but try saying it twen-ty-five times quickly. The point is, that whether we technical-ly take a break every 90 to 120 minutes, we nevertheless, take unconscious breaks. We yawn, daydream, lose concentration, or "zone out" into a trance-like state, where our mind is any-where but on our work. Rossi suggests taking a break in which you lie down if possible, or at least sit comfortably and view a restful scene.

Using Ultradian Breaks

Access the deeper breath, advises Rossi. Many people's minds are on red alert, and they become very uncomfortable doing nothing. Rossi also suggests using spontaneous fantasy, memory, daydreaming, any type of mind wandering, for exam-ple, going on vacation or taking a hike through mountains or meadows. Review a real life experience that is comforting. Eat a light snack (200-300 calories) before you relax. Do not listen to self-help tapes, or read; darken lights if possible. After 15-20 minutes, you should feel refreshed and rejuvenated. Rossi points out that an Ultradian break is different from a nap, because afterwards, you will feel comfortable and alert. An actual sleep nap drops your brain waves into a state that can produce sluggishness, or a slightly groggy feeling. The Ultradian state, in brain wave activity, is somewhere between consciousness and sleep. Rossi maintains that unlike a nap, there is usually no residual sluggish feeling with these types of breaks. Instead, you should feel relaxed, with a clear sense of refreshment.

To manage the low points of our days, Rossi

Taking Breaks to Rejuvenate

1. Every 90 to 120 minutes, our body cycles through an Ulradian Rhythm, periods of heightened physical and mental awareness; our body then signals for a break.
2. Sit quietly and view a restful scene, either physically, or mentally, as in a hike through the woods. Breath deeply.
3. Eat a light snack, and do not read, or listen to tapes-- you want your brain wave activity to be somewhere between consciousness and sleep.
4. Take breaks every 90 to 120 minutes to keep alertness from dropping.

suggests monitoring our "breaking points" where our alertness drops off abruptly. Use these times to insert an Ultradian break, and check to see if it improves your overall work performance.

Tie-In to Success

How many times do you catch yourself muttering: "When I get caught up... I'll do it when I have more time; followed by, There's never enough time!" Or, "I know I should spend more time, but..." All these morose statements indicate that you're not pleased with the way your time is allotted. At the end of a day, how do you determine if you spent your time wisely? Perhaps you gauge it by items crossed off your To Do List; or you may judge it simply by a feeling of accomplishment, a kind of internal click that's activated by high priority accomplishments. Some individuals believe they simply never get enough done. It's as if time and the person are engaged in some primordial battle that of course, time is winning.

Success and Ambition Attitudes

If you're battling time on a regular basis, and believe you're losing the skirmishes, you may want to question whether you're fighting your attitudes toward success and ambition. It's difficult to carve out an individual philosophy of what success means to you. Often success and ambition get tangled up in society's expectations, and individuals lose sight of what is personally fulfilling for them.

Many career strategists believe that a prodrome, or early warning signals of approaching success is the feeling that your life is in

> ## Tie-in to Success
>
> 1. Does your life maintain a balance between routine and spontaneity?
> 2. How many times a week can you juggle some impromptu pleasant activities into your everyday routine?
> 3. Delegate, simplify, eliminate, modify, and streamline activities that eat up your time!

pieces and that you, as a person, are moving in umpteen different directions. "Great," you think, "that describes my life everyday." The critical factor is whether your time and life are more fragmented than integrated. If you suffer from frustration and aggravation because you can't accomplish all you set out to do, then you need to question whether your life and time are truly integrated. The second issue is: are your expectations for achievement realistic?

Finding the Balance

Your life may be intrinsically satisfying, but parts of it are out of kilter. Does your job and personal life maintain a balance of routine and spontaneity? Even frantically busy people can be in a rut and not derive any satisfactions from their accomplishments.

Can you jazz up your daily routine? Can you leave some breathing space for spontaneity? Occasionally, you simple have to figure time in for impulsive behavior, like stopping to feed ducks at a pond, on the way home from running errands. If your schedule is so tightly packed, that you can't ever be impulsive, then you'll eventually feel like your day runs like a railroad time schedule – no time for unscheduled stops.

Keeping On Track

To further integrate your time and strive for balance, you have to monitor your time regularly. Do you perform some tasks like Pavlov's pups, and never stop to assess whether your time could be spent more productively? Weed out tasks that gobble up your time, delegate, simplify, eliminate, modify, or streamline. To achieve balance in your life, your time activities need to be evaluated on a daily basis, otherwise time will be controlling you.

Cracking Your Energy Code

You have the energy level of a bowl of tapioca. Unfortunately, you need to get some serious work done, and you find your concentration level non-existent. Why does it seem that vegetative states seem to coincide with work rushes? It may not be your imagination, it may be your individual "energy code". Researchers have always been fascinated with the question of energy. Why are there high-energy people who never seem to run down, and the opposite, the slugs of society? It doesn't seem fair. Current research seems to indicate that energy is not just a physical factor, but involved in emotional rhythms as well.

Two Body Cycles: Energy and Tension

Robert E. Thayer, author of *The Biopsychology of Mood and Arousal* believes that there are two body wide systems: an energy cycle and a tension cycle. Thayer notes that the way these two cycles pair up determines whether you feel calm energy (when physical vigor is high and emotional tension low) or tense energy (when both physical vigor and emotional tension are high).

Calm Versus Tense Energy

When time is at a premium, we crank out more work when we are under pressure. As a result, most people identify "tense energy" as their most productive time. Actually, the opposite is usually true. Calm energy is associated with enhanced thinking, learning and general intellectual activity. The difference is that tense energy can not be sustained very long; you end up with "tense tiredness" when your body is exhausted but your emotions are still racing. It's akin to racing a sport car's engine up on blocks.

Deciphering Your Energy Code

To crack your energy code, experts recommend charting your energy peaks on a daily basis. You'll notice that your peaks and slumps have a fairly predictable pattern over a typical week. Perhaps you go full steam all day, but your energy levels begin crashing late in the afternoon. Try matching your high concentration work to your peak times, and see if you don't maximize your time management.

> ### Cracking Your Energy Code
>
> 1. Chart your energy peaks – highs and lows.
> 2. Match high concentration work to peak energy times.
> 3. Save energy slumps for low priority tasks.

Be aware that it's difficult to arrange work times and peak times simultaneously, but being cognizant of your most energetic moments can help you plan your time.

Reacting to Time Stimuli

A California psychologist has determined that there are two very distinct ways of responding to time stimuli; you are either a high screener or a low screener. Low screeners have super-efficient nervous systems, and respond rapidly; under stress and time shortages, they tend to get frazzled nerves. Dr. Albert Mehrabian, at the University of California, Los Angeles, developed questions to determine your sensitivity to arousal. "Were you a good baby?" An affirmative answer may mean you're a high screener, along with a tendency to doggedly pursue goals. High screeners usually push themselves to complete projects, and exhibit few procrastinating ways. What does this have to do with your babyhood foibles? Good babies were usually the ones who could sleep through a Kansas tornado, and were not very susceptible to cold, heat, or hunger. The payoff of these high-screening traits is that as adults, individuals are less susceptible to changes in environment, distractions, and other people's interruptions.

Reacting to Time Stimuli

1. Low Screeners get easily distracted, and easily bored. They face a tough time getting themselves out of time swamps. The more frantic it gets, the more frenzied they become.
2. High screeners are less susceptible to outside stimuli, and find it easier to keep on track with priorities.
3. Sometimes a physical change in environment will lower sensory input and lessen overload for low screeners.

Low Screener Traits

Low screeners, on the other hand, because of their higher arousal level, tend to be ambitious self-starters on jobs, but become bored easily. Because of their enthusiasm, and tendency to over-commit themselves, low screeners may quickly suffer from work overload. Since they are more readily subject to their emotions, low screeners are very capable of rationalizing to themselves that they're simply too depressed to work on the boring quarterly reports. A dreary, rainy day may make them restless, and put them even further behind in managing their time.

Strategies for High and Low Screeners

What are some pointers for the high screener and the low screener in regard to time use? A low screener needs "permission" for non-productive, goof-off time. It may be exactly what they need to become less frazzled, as well as gain distance from job overload. The high screener, born with discipline, fortitude, and 23 other types of virtues, has no problem saying no to requests, or to setting priorities. Low screeners usually need to stop the cycle of events that are leading them into frantic, frazzled activity; sometimes physically removing themselves from a work area, and forcing a change in environment will lower sensory input.

Whether you are a high or low screener, it makes sense that many time management issues are intricately tied in with the amount of stimuli that bombard your mind every few seconds. If nothing else, at your next social gathering, ask the person next to you if low noises bother them. It's no, for a low screener. Were they good babies? Yes, for a high screener.

Overwork and Time

Are you suffering from "jet lag", and you haven't been any-where near a plane? Are you sullen, angry, depressed, and resent-ful about the hours you put in at work – and sullen and depressed doesn't normally describe your personality? More than occasionally, do you feel that your life has lost its savor, that it's out of balance? Do friends and family complain about being neglected? You may be suffering from the career track blues. In the early 1990s, career psychologists began to notice a common phenomenon among hard workers in various corporations. It wasn't merely that people were working hard and long hours; that seems to be the terrain of most companies in lean and mean times. Rather, it was apparent that many employees across com-panies were feeling that they couldn't accomplish enough; bedev-iling feelings were emerging that success and hard work was not paying off in job satisfaction or reward.

Hard Work Versus Overwork

Hard work, of course, is not a career pitfall. Research indi-cates that hard work alone, does not seem to have long-term deleterious effects. It is the distinction between working long and hard, and feeling chronically overloaded that is critical. Individuals can push the perimeters of hard work and physical endurance, particularly at various career points: starting a new job, building a new business, or trying to get an important work project off and running. Overworking, on the other hand, is a pattern of psychological addiction to work. Dr. Bryan E. Robinson, author of *Chained to the Desk* (New York University Press, 1998) notes that over workers feel inadequate, regardless of their accomplishments, and they constantly set higher, impossible goals to reach.

The irony of overwork, is that the long term effect of working too much is that over-doing workers may evolve into a cycle of low functioning at work, which has repercussions for their eventual performance reviews. Usually, the work style of overworking individuals is not very conducive to team playing, as they are not too adept at negotiating and being flexible about different ideas. As supervisors over workers are often loathe to delegate as they don't trust the working styles of others; as a result, they fall even further behind. Their stress level, which is already high from overwork, will be raised even higher by negative feedback about their job performance. As a result, overworking individuals feel even more overwhelmed, and out of control.

Overwork and Time

1. Ask for help to cope with an overwhelming work load. The most successful leaders ask for help from peers, co-workers, and even bosses.
2. Shore up your mutual help network. Build alliances and utilize others expertise and consultation.
3. Set boundaries as to how many work hours you will allot to your job. Keep to these boundaries, and ask family and friends to remind you of your promises.
4. Find hobbies and outlets that are not structured, competitive, and schedule-ridden. You don't want to replicate the pressures of work with a leisure interest.

Stress Relief for Overwork

There are some practical remedies to cope with the seemingly endless cycle of overwork, as well as the frustration of trying to control a workload. The first is to realize that your work style is causing problems. Robinson points out that most overworking individuals blame their problems on their company, the economy, the current lifestyle, or their need for a paycheck; they rarely see that they have a choice in the way they work. The first step then, is to take responsibility for the work schedules.

Second, over workers need to set boundaries for the number of hours worked, and stick to those guidelines. Boundaries might include sticking to an eight hour day; not working weekends, or bringing work on vacation time.

Third, learn to ask for help at work. Research on superior managers found that they asked for advice and help much more frequently (from peers, and subordinates), than did less promotable managers. Superior managers built mutual-help networks in the organization. They also used the resources of the organization to help accomplish projects. They used consultants and technical assistants to avoid duplicating work, as well as to provide understanding and expertise on complex projects.

Fourth, over workers, according to Robinson, need to learn to blend work with play and labor with leisure, rather than let work and play be polar opposites in their lives. Robinson states that it's important that over workers choose a hobby, sport, or pastime that they will do imperfectly. Right-brain activities such as art, dancing, or acting can take workaholics out of their serious, logical, left-sided brain activities and give them experiences with the creative, intuitive, right side of the brain.

Forge ahead and derail yourself from the career track syndrome.

Beating Work Burnout

Every October 12th celebrates "International Moment of Frustration Scream Day." The observers of this event urge "all citizens of the world to go outdoors at twelve hundred hours Greenwich time and scream for 30 seconds. We will feel better, or Earth will go off its orbit," according to the Low Thresholders of the Earth League.

No doubt we all feel like screaming when our time gets out of control. The most stressful times seem to be when we're operating in "hamster mode;" we're just spinning our exercise wheels, and not getting anywhere.

Two Routes to Frustration

Two factors increase our frustration levels: the first is to be constantly busy, but not feel any progress. The second factor is a lack of reward or sense of accomplishment for what we have done. When we are listing our day's priorities, necessities, and "grass-catcher" items, we need to pay attention to what comprises our lists.

We think we can identify our priorities readily. But the essential question about a priority is simply, how important is it, compared to our other lurking priorities? Is the task a priority because it fits in with long-term goals or objectives? Is the task a priority because it is a maintenance function and you're buying time in the future? For example, by keeping your car serviced, you are hoping it will remain reliable some blustery winter morning.

More Priority Questions

The next question to ask about priorities is how much time are you willing to assign to the completion of the task?

Sometimes the time estimation, alone helps us sift and balance our priorities immediately. Priorities also need to be considered in both long-term and short-term time frames; they need deadlines, and they need to be tracked at regular intervals to make certain they're current.

Two Routes to Time Disaster

Remember, crisis management and shifting priorities to lower status are two of the easiest ways to spin your wheels like a frenetic hamster. There is always a temptation to concentrate on lower status priorities because they are often easier to do, they may be more fun, or worse, you may mistake lower status tasks for high priority items.

Priority Determination

Ask yourself where priorities fit in a four-square grid. Are they: important and urgent; important but not urgent; urgent but not important; or neither important or urgent. Use this determination to assign a priority code to all the items on your daily to-do list. If you have to make decisions about priorities every day, it will become very clear where your time is really spent. You may be caught in a "busyness"

Beating Work Burnout

1. Crisis management and shifting our priorities to lower status are two prime ways we lose traction with time.
2. If you are concentrating on lower status priority items you will certainly be busy, but missing will be a feeling of accomplishment and satisfaction.
3. Re-order your priorities:
   · important and urgent
   · important but not urgent
   · urgent but not important
   · neither important or urgent

---

trap. You can account for your time, but it's focused on low priority items in your work life or home. You may have inadvertently assigned a low priority status to activities that could give you a sense of accomplishment or achievement. It's time to turn those priorities around. While you're at it, practice your 30-second frustration scream.

Juggling Tasks: Multi-Tasking Skills

"Multi-tasking" has been added to our lexicon by way of computer technology: we can have several tasks in process at the same time. Harried parents, chauffeuring their brood to sports practice, have children eating pizza in the back seat, while in the front seat, they're quizzing their fourth grader on vocabulary words—multi-tasking, once again. Doing a number of tasks at the same time has always been a time management standard. Time and efficiency studies have always tested the limits of human behavior to increase production time. As America became increasingly, more industrialized, anything "efficient, scientific, and modern" became synonymous with value. If any task could be done faster, we assume it's an improvement. But is it?

Focusing On Our Tasks

In managing our time, are we better off doing a number of tasks simultaneously? Computers are wired to do it, but should we mimic our computer? The answer is probably best determined by our individual ability to juggle tasks and focus concentration.

Pinpoint your preferences; if you get bored easily, chances are, you're hopscotching from task to task, anyway. Perhaps, you've discovered you work best in short bursts of time; you thrive when you allow yourself to vary your routine. The goal, then, for the task juggler, is to establish significant progress on a task, rather than applying just bits and pieces of time in a slapshot fashion. If your style is to keep multiple projects going, then you just need to apply some structure so you don't lose sight of your goals.

Three strategies that are critical for the task juggler are: planning time, scheduling regular task time, and allowing creative think-time. If you are juggling multiple tasks, anticipation and planning skills will set the foundation for your multitasking. Planning out the project, with action steps and deadlines will save about thirty percent of your actual clock time. Anticipation skills force you to think about the pre-tasks that are necessary for your plans. Do you need to order supplies, data, or schedule personnel, or appointments. Jot down a list of quick tasks that will get the project moving; the quick tasks as serve as quick motivational tools as well.

Think Creatively

Creative thinking time is essential for the task jug-

Juggling Tasks

1. Determine if you are a task juggler, or a task focuser? Pinpointing your work preference can help you be more efficient.
2. The task juggler, who hopscotches from task to task needs to create some structure to keep sight of goals: planning, scheduling regular task work, and allowing time for creative thought.
3. Planning, with time lines and action plans will save about 30% of your clock time.
4. Successful multi-tasking requires monitoring your task at regular intervals, as well as checking on follow-up activities.

gler; if you're in and out of tasks too quickly, you may be overlooking creative ways to approach the task. You need to focus on what creativity consultant Roger von Oech calls a good dose of soft thinking in the germinal phase of a project, and a hearty helping of hard thinking in the practical phase.

Multi-tasking requires monitoring the project at various points to gauge its progress, as well as follow-up activities.

Sleep Time

You've seen the types. You lament that you've been up since dawn working like an adrenaline crazed weasel. Without an eyelash flicker, your companions casually mention that they're always at their computers by 4 AM, everyday. Famous writers, known for their yearly 900 page opus, admit they customarily create at a 3 AM. You wonder, how do they go without sleep? Sure, you might be at your computer at 3 AM., but you would be unconscious and uncombed.

Power Sleep

Sleep reduction has become the latest one-upmanship in time management. Historically, many geniuses and highly creative people have been short sleepers. Albert Schweitzer reportedly slept three hours per day, and Thomas Edison clocked in at four hours, and often stated that people who spent a great deal of time sleeping were fools. (Albert Einstein, conversely, belonged to the contingent of geniuses who believed in sleeping late!) Oprah, and other current celebrities have bragged about their skimpy sleep schedules. Major national magazine articles and books have been published on the benefits of sleep reduction. If you cut back two hours of sleep each week, suggests one writer, you'll gain 14 hours extra a week — one extra long workday!

Current Sleep Research

Before you start salivating about your extra day in the week, let's look at what the experts say. Studies reported by Dr. Peretz Lavie, Dean of the Faculty of Medicine at the Technion-Israel Institute of Technology in Israel, and head of the Sleep Laboratory, reports that persons who cut down their sleep pay a price: they have increased sleepiness during the day. Dr. Lavie notes that individuals may explicitly deny any ill effects from sleep deprivation. Very young adults, particularly, suffer from chronic deep debt. Sleeping late on weekends, and napping during the day, maintains Dr. Lavie, indicates that individuals are not enjoying luxurious sleep, but attempting to keep sleep accounts balanced.

Sleep Deprivation

Researchers estimate that the majority of Americans get between 60 and 90 minutes less sleep than they should. In fact, you know it's become a real problem when Congress funded a comprehensive sleep study. If everyone can stay awake, we'll probably benefit from the results.

Sleep Time

1. Stop pushing your sleep barriers as a way of garnering extra time. Find your personal sleep pattern and stick to it.
2. Chronic sleep deprivation results in lowered creativity the very next day.
3. Try adding an extra hour of sleep for a week and then decide if you're more efficient throughout the day. If you must shorten sleep, cut back 10 to 15 minutes every week and monitor your well-being. Add more sleep if you're edgy or irritable.

Saving Time Or Sleep?

What has propelled the short-sleep cycle mystique as a way to save time? Time management experts estimate that everyone could be about 20% more effective by streamlining their daily routines. To grab your 20%, you need to manage your time differently. Most individuals rationalize that first, they can't do it; and/or, (2) they don't want to do it; and/ or, they are currently pushing their own time barriers, as it is. Studies indicate that career women already sleep 5% less than their male counterparts and are too close to the biological edge to cut back any further. Researchers Webb and Agnew (1975) found that cutting back sleep time by about two hours for two months produced no major behavioral consequences. They concluded that a few hours of transient, or even chronic sleep loss from work requirements, personality disorders, or insomnia, were not likely to result in major behavioral consequences.

Readjusting Your Sleep Patterns

If you still look to shortened sleep as a way of cadging more time, experts suggest finding your personal sleep pattern. Adjust your sleep by 10-15 minutes a night until you feel at your best. Do this gradually, since, for most people the biological edge of sleep is six hours; the ideal is between seven and eight hours.

There is a price to be paid for shortening sleep: going without sleep for just one night diminishes our ability to think creatively the next day, cautions James A. Horne, Ph.D. a British sleep researcher. If you do lose sleep, it will take several weeks of satisfying sleep to catch up.

Sleep reduction may not be the ideal time saver. If everyone seems snarly to you, and your co-workers suggest a personality implant, you probably need more sleep. Take a nap and think about it.

CHAPTER 3

Procrastination

Symptoms of Procrastination

Why do people procrastinate? The puzzling answer is that procrastination occurs for over twenty different reasons, and that's precisely why it is so difficult to assess and eliminate. Time experts have defined procrastination differently, but the one consensus is that procrastination is both a combination of guilt and postponing tasks.

Procrastination Reasons

We can procrastinate because we're feeling confused or overwhelmed by a task; so we simply put our energy into avoiding the task. We can procrastinate because we're miffed with someone – a supervision or co-worker, so we take out our anger by never getting around to the task. We can also procrastinate with the twin monsters of time, obsessiveness and perfectionism. Or, we can simply procrastinate because we're depressed, bored, or angry.

Delay Tactics

Analyze your reasons for delaying. If you can play detective and ferret out a pattern in the postponement of a job, you'll recognize your symptoms sooner. List all your reasons for not doing a job. (Yes, this seems patently ridiculous, but after all, you're not exactly doing the task anyway!) Note the environmental conditions as well: it's raining, the copier machine has the vapors, you're too tired to walk to the accounting department, and so on. You may see a continuous trend emerging here. Maybe your danger times are early in the morning, and your sluggish start sets the pace early in the day. Maybe you crawl to a stop after lunch, the infamous "siesta time". Office experts tell us the most productive day of the week is Tuesday, for obvious reasons.

Beginning, Middle or End of a Task?

Look at the "when" of procrastination. Do you procrastinate at the beginning, middle or end of a task? You may believe that you are creative and eclectic and procrastinate all three ways, but you may actually veer towards a procrastination preference.

> ## Symptoms of Procrastination
>
> 1. Look at why you're procrastinating: ferret out all your reasons.
> 2. Identify when you procrastinate:
>   At the beginning of a task: suspect boredom, fear, or lack of knowledge on where to begin. Devise strategies to reduce the risk, increase your knowledge base
>   The middle of a task? Sprinkle in some rewards and benchmarks to keep you moving.
>   The end: Every week set aside a short block of time to just finish up odds and ends.
> 3. Repeat to yourself: I finish things fully.

If you procrastinate at the beginning of a task, suspect boredom or confusion. Make a fast list of steps to complete the task. If you don't know how to even begin tackling the task, then your procrastination may be an intermingling of fear and risks that are inhibiting you. If you suspect boredom as a root of procrastinating, brainstorm a way to make the task more intrinsically interesting or pleasurable.

In the Middle of A Task

For the middle of the task procrastinator, the thrill is gone. The initial rush of beginning a task has dimmed, and ennui is setting in. Some times the "buddy system" helps here, as another person can add commitment and interest. If your task has to be a solitary task, sandwich it in between two pleasurable tasks. (Of course, this is self-bribery; we're not saints, we're procrastinators.)

At the End of A Task

For the procrastinator at the end of a task, you can recognize your behavior easily: you have more than five unfinished tasks hovering about like homeless phantoms. Your bill-paying checks might be written out, but not mailed for four days. Your cleaning bundle makes it to the trunk of your car, but not the cleaners. The end procrastinator is in need of a hour set aside each week for clean-up on leftover tasks; by consolidating them all in a solid bloc, tasks have a better chance of getting finished.

Who ever said procrastination was simple?

Procrastination Ploys

New research indicates that 80% of the population indulges in procrastination; the other 20% probably put off answering the survey! Procrastinators often exhibit a lethal combination of overdoing and busyness. One of the striking similarities among procrastinators is that they often insist that they need huge amounts of undisturbed time to tackle "important work." Procrastinators prefer that conditions be perfect before they tackle work, rather than work in substandard, less optimum ways.

Getting Into a Project

There lies the catch-22 of time management: there is no "right time" to do a project. The reality of managing our time is that we may have to parcel out projects in dibs and dabs. We may not have the time to wait for the right tools, the slant of the moon, or for cosmic inspiration. The difference between procrastinators and individuals who get things done is that procrastinators often start on the easiest tasks first. They then become seduced by busywork—routine tasks that they can finish in the shortest time available. Being busy and churning out small jobs makes the procrastinator feel virtuous, but the doesn't solve the larger problem of undone tasks.

Changing Habits: Strategy One

There are some specific behavioral changes that can help with procrastination. First, break important tasks into brief, daily segments. You can even make tasks as brief as ten or fifteen minutes, as long as you finish them. Add these tasks up over a week's time; you'll probably find they give you a more substantial investment than concentrated periods.

Strategy Two

Second, jump in and begin work. Procrastinators often wait for a internal signal of willingness to tackle a task: it may be your favorite delaying tactic. You can begin a task without having the burning desire to start on it.

Behavioral Changes to Combat Procrastination

1. Break important tasks into brief, daily segments. (You will probably not have large chunks of uninterrupted time!)
2. Jump into a task and begin. (Procrastinators often wait for the right moment, or a sign from the cosmos!)
3. Set a time limit on the task.
4. Put some fun into the task (Use music, treats, and breaks.)
5. Reward yourself as the task progresses. Encourage even small successes.

Strategy Three

Third, set a limit on how time you devote to a task. Procrastinators, once started on a task, can often overdo, and burn themselves out on a project. Stick to your original time promises; don't overextend your time.

Strategy Four

Fourth, try to put in some pleasure into the task. Procrastinators earn negative energy by pairing postponed tasks with levels of stress. When procrastinators think about the various odd tasks they are ignoring, they usually feel waves of mild, to moderate stress. Figure out ways to add fun, and increase stretch breaks throughout the day.

Strategy Five

Five, encourage yourself with small successes. Use graph paper to block out completed tasks, or use lists. Buy yourself small treats as goal markers. Lastly, don't isolate yourself; it heightens the feeling of being "punished" by a task. Try to turn a task into something more social, or increase your social excursions. Acquire a running or exercise partner, check in with a work friend about a task, make contracts with others, but get some help to reinforce new behavior. Don't let procrastination be, as writer Don Marquis observed, "The art of keeping up with yesterday."

Instant Procrastination Excuses

Procrastination workshops were offered in California, and had to be canceled – no one signed up until the last minute. In a book on procrastination, California psychologists Jane Burka, and Lenora Yuen used their introduction to thank Federal Express: "Without whom we would have missed numerous last-minute deadlines."

Defining Procrastination

Procrastination affects people in all job descriptions, personalities, and lifestyles. Often, there's even the question of whether one is actually procrastinating, or is there simply too much to do in the time allotted? Procrastination is defined as the behavior of postponing tasks. The difference between everyday procrastination, which everyone indulges in, and debilitating procrastination, is the amount of havoc the procrastination brings to your life.

Procrastination Excuses

Chances are, procrastination symptoms usually first appear when you're on the verge of starting a project, or toying with the idea of putting it off. Your excuses will become wonderfully creative; your imagination can soar when you're dredging up an airtight, logical, and rational reason for procrastinating. Often, excuses for postponing tasks appear so rapidly and automatically that pet excuses are seldom even analyzed. What are your favorite excuses?

So you don't have to put off thinking about your most

popular procrastination excuses, here are some classics:

· I'm too tired now; I'll do it later.

· I don't have enough time to do it all now, so there's no point in starting.

· I can't work with such a messy desk; I'll have to straighten it up first.

Additional Excuses

Other excuses might be telling yourself you've been working hard, and deserve to goof off. Or, you'll wait until you feel inspired, for the weather to get better, or you'll wait until you have the proper equipment.(In some organizations that could mean a very long wait!)

Consider: It's too late in the week to get started. Whatever is on your laundry list of excuses, it may be helpful for you to keep track of them for a week or so. Pay attention to what happened before you dredged up your excuses. Were you particularly bored, tired, restless, or anxious? Procrastination occurs for a multitude of reasons. Remember, the goal of your excuse-collecting is to

Instant Procrastination Excuses

1. Is procrastination a problem? The determinining factor is the amount of havoc that procrastination bring to your life.
2. Procrastination excuses start cropping up when you are subconsciously toying with the idea of postponing a task.
3. Keep track of your excuses for procrastination for a week or two.
4. Good time managers see obstacles as barriers to barge through. Procrastinators view barriers as proof they should postpone a task.

simply observe your behavior around procrastination ploys. You may even give yourself the luxury of watching your actions for a few weeks to gather a good analysis of how your rationalize your behavior.

Analyzing Alibis

The point of looking at your alibis for procrastination is that your excuses may be valid: you may have had a tough day at the gizmo factory, but is that a good enough excuse to keep you from starting a project? Remember the true function of procrastination excuses are to get you to avoid something. You almost have to believe your own excuses, or they would lost their power to convince you that you can goof off a bit. Never mind, that you'll hate yourself and your excuses in the morning—the excuses are working!

Characteristics of Effective Time Managers

The difference between procrastinators and effective time managers is that good time managers don't allow a difficulty to stop them from a task. They can forge ahead, despite less than ideal situations; procrastinators will stop dead in their tracks at the first sniff of difficulty. Effective time managers consider what can be done, and get started, while procrastinators remain flipping through their card file of excuses.

Battling Procrastination

Procrastination is derived from the Latin, "pro", meaning "forward," and crastinate, "until tomorrow." Since time immemorial, researchers have been puzzled about how to describe procrastinators. Some have said, diplomatically, that "procrastinators suffer from a time urgency," probably somewhat akin to describing Dr. Jekyll as having mood swings.

Other researchers have characterized procrastinators as "undisciplined, careless and disorderly." If that wasn't damning enough, the researchers also believed that they were timid, lacked confidence, and suffered from anxiety. They didn't add it, but they probably found they parked in two spaces, and littered, as well. Naturally, these dreadful characteristics doesn't describe you, but rather those other procrastinators, who, of course, are textbook models of neuroses.

Two Factors in Procrastination

In *How to Get Out of a Rut*, Dr. William J. Knaus (Prentice-Hall, 1982), believes that procrastination has two factors in common; what he calls "self-doubt downing" and "discomfort dodging." Self doubt occurs, and often centers around your abilities to begin a project; sometimes the doubt revolves around the eventual success of a project. For example, you know you could accomplish more if you organized your paperwork files; but what a boring, and overwhelming job! The next, psychological step in self-doubt downing is you begin to experience discomfort fear, and, in order to avoid the discomforting feelings, you procrastinate. As a result, you start engaging in poor "self-organizing", or putting things off, and, as a result you end up with increased negative conclusions about yourself. To avoid feeling tense, you pursue low priority tasks, and avoid the tougher, more complicated tasks. The result: you get further and further behind.

The Complex Side of Procrastination

Now, of course, procrastination is not always so simple. Practitioners have devised wonderfully complex, diversionary ploys. Any war tactician will agree that diversionary ploys have to be believable to work. The easiest ploy to believe is that tomorrow or next week, will be a better time for an activity; perhaps, you'll be in a better mood, or have more preparation time. This "manana" attitude, of course, doesn't result in well-prepared tasks performed in a superb mood; it simply results in a false sense of security that a task will eventually get done. It is "discomfort dodging" at its best.

Breaking Through Self Doubt and Discomfort Dodging

To break out of this cyclical pattern of "self- doubt downing" and "discomfort dodging," Dr. Knaus suggests writing down any self-doubts that contribute to the procrastination, such as "I can't act until I'm certain," or "I'll never be able to finish this job."

Pinpoint Low Frustration Messages

Next, identify the low frustration tolerance language you use, that goes along with your procrastination activities, such as "I don't feel like it," or "This task will bore me to death." For the next step, pinpoint your specific diversionary tactics and try to short circuit them. If you get captivated by the TV on your way to work on your taxes, turn it off, or avoid the room, but be aware that you're in danger of being diverted by an old, ingrained habit.

Focusing on the Task

Take a hard look at your current procrastinated task. Are you telling yourself that lack the skill to begin the task? Or, are you setting up certain standards, for example, the task has to be completed rapidly and perfectly? After this analysis, you need to decide on a course of action that will sustain your counter-procrastination program.

Battling Procrastination

1. Write down any self-doubting statements.
2. Listen to your low-frustration tolerance language, such as:
   I don't feel like it, now.
   I can't get started now.
3. Identify your diversionary tactics and short circuit them.
4. Find some strategies to keep your counter-procrastination program going.

Five Steps To End Procrastination

"Life," observed writer Henry Miller, "as it is called, is for most of us one long postponement." If procrastination is hampering your time management efforts, you've already learned how creative you can be about procrastinating. Procrastination is not simple, but rather a complex set of behaviors. When we're busy putting off something, we don't stop and analyze: "Obviously, I'm not working on the weekly reports because of deeply buried feelings of autonomy, power and hidden resentments toward my boss." You may garner wonderful insights about your intricate machinations, but such armchair analysis won't actually spur you on to accomplishing the task. To start moving on procrastination, it's helpful to follow a five point plan.

First, pick one particular area of procrastination that needs some work. A concrete example might be to begin compiling Friday's weekly reports by Wednesday afternoon. Notice, you're not trying to tackle your entire work and home life, but rather one discrete entity.

Step two is to set a regularly scheduled time to complete this task. Many tasks are ear-marked for procrastination because they can be postponed with few warning signals. Allotting a regular time slot to a task cuts back on the probability of postponing it. Think about television shows: the network's kiss of death to a program is to move it from its regular time slot — viewers can't find it, and settle for other programs to fill in the vacuum. The same principle happens when you become creative with the time to complete a task. Remember the old English proverb: "One of these days is none of these days."

The third step in battling procrastination is to create "instant tasks". Time management expert, Edwin Bliss labels it the "salami method". Take your task and slice into pieces, then attack one of the "salami slices". Bliss says, "Promise yourself that you won't force yourself to get involved with the main job, provided you do at least one of the small steps on your list."

The fourth step is to set a deadline for your task.

> **Five Point Plan to Tackle Procrastination**
>
> 1. Pick one area of procrastination to tackle.
> 2. Set a regular time to work on this task.
> 3. Create instant tasks; do one small part toward the task.
> 4. Set a deadline.
> 5. Complete the task and reward yourself liberally!

If you're an adrenaline junkie, then you know the thrill of a heavy, breathing, deadline acts as a motivator. Many procrastinated tasks simply don't get done because they're too amorphous and have no set time. For example, cleaning your gutters is admirable, but it's a task that can be postponed until heavy snow makes it impossible. Then The True Procrastinator's Lament can be heard: "I was just about to get to those gutters...oh well, next spring." A deadline focuses concentration and energy on a task. Sometimes a deadline is all the motivation you need for some tasks.

Finally, when you've completed the dreaded task, reward

yourself. It doesn't matter how long you've dragged your feet, you still deserve to celebrate breaking through your own procrastination. Start today.

Procrastination and Priorities

You've mastered the "fine art of procrastination." Procrastination is bad, or course, and priorities are good. But using procrastination effectively can help you manage your time.

Procrastination Strategies

From Time Management 101, and the 587 time articles, you've ingested, you know that priorities are simply value-laden tasks. If you've even had one of those days that you'd swear you'd been in a time warp—the day just vanished, it was probably due to having the day over-filled with low priority tasks that gobbled up your time. Procrastinating effectively on low priority tasks is the key to accomplishing more of what you want. Some other strategies that are effective are flexibility, good "grass-catcher" lists, deadlines and concentration.

Building Flexibility

"If only I wasn't interrupted so much, I could ..." rebuild the Holy Roman Empire, find the cure for lateness, and so on. Most of us lament having to respond to other's crises, emergencies and instant demands. In reality, interruptions are going to occur, and none of us will ever be able to adhere religiously to our To Do lists, as we'd like. If you don't build flexibility into your daily schedule, you'll be doomed for time management frustration.

Grass-catcher Lists

A good "grass-catcher" list is defined as low-priority items that probably need to be done. They don't belong on a list with high priority items, because they are the tasks that you may be able to procrastinate around. "Grass-catcher" items may be marginal, or they may be significant, so they need a separate list. They're very much like the mulch that your lawnmower catches.

Installing Deadlines

Deadlines are essential for procrastination. Amazingly, we often tend to meet other's deadlines, but may fall into the habit of not asking or negotiating deadlines from others. Deadlines create a sense of urgency for high priority tasks, both with yourself and others. Don't bother to assign deadlines to low-priority tasks. To procrastinate effectively, you have to remove the sense of urgency from all trivial tasks.

Keeping Focused

Lastly, marshal your powers of concentration. Use the time that you feel sharpest intellectually, on your high priority tasks. Don't let someone else's agenda eat up your premium concentration hours.

Procrastination and Priorities

1. If you have to procrastinate, put off your low priority tasks.
2. Build flexibility into your daily schedule, or you will be using interruptions as good reasons for procrastinating.
3. Set aside some grass-catcher time to clean up odds and ends of tasks.
4. Set deadlines for high priority tasks.
5. Concentrate; go after your high priority tasks when you are at your sharpest—both intellectually and physically.

Procrastinate, and respond to other's requests, when you're not wasting your peak concentration time.

Learning to procrastinate effectively helps you gain more control over your time. Don't put it off; begin today to fine-tune your procrastination skills.

Great Escapes To Procrastination

You've been meaning to clean your basement, closets, or fill-in-the-blank for weeks, now. Somehow, it just gets postponed. Yet, you're busy and active, and can't quite figure where the time goes. You may be using a great escape. Great escapes are those activities which move you away from your number one priorities. They may take the form of socializing, indulging yourself, reading, doing a task yourself instead of delegating, overdoing it, or running away.

Wonderful, you muse, you use all these excuses, and, sometimes on the same day. Obviously, the list of great escapes sounds like a wish list from some pathetic drudge who needs de-stressing immediately. How much socializing do you do per work day? Visiting various work cubicles Indulging yourself sounds very therapeutic and rewarding, but how often do you use it as an escape route?

The Reading Escape

You tell yourself that reading is great for your soul, and who can resist the lure of an engrossing book? But, does reading serve to keep you away from beginning a project? Just 794 more pages of *War and Peace*, and you'll mow the lawn, you lie to yourself.

Doing Everything Yourself

Doing it yourself is another great escape. It can run the gamut from not using available resources, to making a task so cumbersome no one else could possibly help. For example, making three trips to the grocery store a week, instead of one trip eats up your schedule and wrecks havoc on your food budget.(The longer you spend in a store, the more dollars you spend on impulse items.) The lack of planning involved keeps the task squarely in your domain, and limits any possible delegation.

Overdoing Tasks

Other escape routes include overdoing, and running away. In overdoing, you may over supervise, and over control tasks. You may adhere to such perfectionistic standards that no one can assist with the task. Other forms of overdoing might be extending meetings and appointments. You may have gotten in the habit of keeping every visitor an extra ten minutes, or extending phone calls. Perhaps you

Six Fast Routes to Procrastination

1. Socializing
2. Indulging yourself.
3. Reading.
4. Doing it yourself.
5. Overdoing.
6. Running away.

practice additional habits that you characterize as attention to detail, but may be, in fact, simple overdoing of a task.

Running Away

Running away is, by far, the easiest escape, and can be practiced on a tiny to a grandiose scale. You can hand-deliver your office memos, take a sudden road trip to the branch office, run errands, or extend your lunch hour; you may not see that you're placing yourself away from your high priority tasks. After all, you rationalize, you cant do your tasks if you're not there. The hidden, and covert goal of running away is obviously to put distance between you and your procrastinated tasks.

Escape Proofing Your Behavior

There is nothing is intrinsically wrong with any of the great escapes; they give life, vitality, and diversion to our daily routines. The great escapes, though, do get us into trouble, however, if they become our subtle, or not so subtle, reasons for not accomplishing the tasks we claim are high priorities. Make certain that your habits don't create surefire escape routes toward procrastination.

Dumping Procrastinated Tasks

We think of Leonardo da Vinci as one of the most cele-
brated artists, inventors, and visionaries of almost any age.
Yet Leonardo had a terrible record of not finishing projects.
When he died, he had more unfinished paintings than finished ones. What would be your legacy to the world in unfinished projects?

Of course, we have all the good, solid reasons for not finishing task: we have more important things to do; aliens ate the
project; or simply, we are going to finish it when we have more
time.

Gaining Closure on Tasks

Face it, the reality is that a great many projects go
undone, simply because we have lost interest in them, they
have little value for us, or the intrinsic payoff for completion
is negligible. One antidote for project hangovers is to gain
some closure on the projects. Make a list of all the orphan
tasks floating around your workplace and home life. Your
most obvious ones will jump out at you, like the prominent
rowing machine in your bedroom that serves as a very expensive coat rack.

Organizing Glitches

Maybe your projects suffer from the out of sight, out of
mind syndrome. If something isn't in plain sight, it vanishes
from your consideration. Organizational experts suggest that
individuals who are highly creative suffer most from the out-

of-sight belief, so creative types tend to keep tabs on projects by keeping everything out. The result is that usually a new problem emerges — disorganized clutter.

Dumping Procrastinated Tasks

1. List all your undone tasks: all the orphan tasks and uncompleted projects.
2. Do some of the tasks represent out-dated values, interests, or hobbies?
3. Give up the guilt, and recycle, give away, or pitch tasks that have little hope of being completed.
4. For the salvageable projects, brainstorm new ways to get them accomplished: use the buddy system, dream up some motivational rewards for yourself, and get closure on them.

After you have listed all your forgotten projects, take an honest look at your list. Do some of the projects represent hobbies or leisure activities in which your interest has waned? How many projects suggest good things for you to do but offer little reward or feeling of satisfaction?

Be truthful. How many of your unfinished projects involve good uses of your time, but not necessarily the best uses of your time? If that's the case, you may have to put some time lines on your project list and admit that some of your unfinished tasks represent ideal tasks and have very little likelihood of being completed — by you, anyway.

Letting Go of Tasks

Unless you are on a massive behavior change program and are really committed to making habit changes, the unfinished tasks will probably remain where they are — unfinished.

Give up on the guilt, give away the reminders of your unfinished tasks and move on the projects that are salvageable.

Upping the Odds for Completing A Task

How can you increase your completion time on salvageable projects? The first way is probably the easiest: use the buddy system. Either physically enlist a friend or colleagues help, or make a contract to report progress to that buddy.

Try offering yourself some rewards or reinforcement to complete the tasks. Determine what you will do for some pleasurable activity. Do you need to break your reward into portions, so that are motivated at various points of the task?

Task efficiency experts tell us that each person probably harbors an affinity for procrastinating on a task at a particular point of the task. Where are the danger signs for your procrastination? Plan some strategies to move through your treacherous times. Do your task, and then schedule your rewards, or bribes accordingly.

CHAPTER 4

Fast Strategies to Cope With Time

Gaining Four Hours of Time

When you are chiding yourself to save time, what kind of time do you envision? Most time management experts believe that almost everyone can streamline their efforts and be more efficient. Would you settle for four hours per week of increased efficiency? Before you scoff, realize that if you work a 40 hour work week, four hours represents 10% of your time. Another way to view it is that four hours is also one week of vacation every ten weeks, five extra weeks of vacation per year, or seventeen more hours per month to spend with your family, or goldfish, or hobbies.

Detecting Your Time

To grab the golden ring of four hours, you have to know where your current time is going. Throughout the years, time management experts have been driven into dithering states because managers simply don't know what they do with their time.

How Managers Spend Time

Pick up any managerial survey, and managers report, straight from a business school textbook, that their functions are managing, delegating, over seeing, planning, budgeting, and other lofty activities, for which they had no time, anyway. By actually watching the behaviors and recording activities, researchers finally figured out how managers really spent their time. Instead of the critical functions managers thought they were performing, instead, their time was spent by frenetic activity, role overload, squandering their energy levels, and fragmentation and superficiality towards job projects. The typical manager engaged in a busy sequence of activities, telephoning, dictating, note-taking, meeting, reading, and talking – all with many interruptions and with very little time for reflection. The average manager was squeezing fourteen hours of work into a compressed eight hour day! The

Working Faster and Doing Less?

1. Cut down on distractions and interruptions.
2. Set priorities.
3. Grab control of paperwork.
4. Use tape recorders and dictating equipment.
5. Review calendar systems daily.
6. Practice better listening skills to cut down on misunderstandings and human error.
7. Brainstorm and harness creativity skills.
8. Practice on-going stress management skills.

result was that because of this fragmented activity, managers often made decisions that were superficial (translation: Bad!), simply because there was no more time to decide.

Eight Steps To Work Smarter

The solution, of course, is never easy, but involves working faster and doing less. The eight steps to working faster are: (1) cut down on distractions and interruptions; (2) set priorities; (3) grab control of your on-going paperwork and develop a system; (4) use tape recorders or dictation equipment; (5) review your calendar or computer system calendar daily; (6) practice better listening skills; (7) set time aside to brainstorm and think creatively; and (8) practice diligent stress management skills.

Three More Time Strategies

To do less involves practicing three additional activities on a daily basis: use good delegation skills, turn down requests and projects that don't add value to your priorities, and keep colleagues from pawning off problems to your desk.

Finding those extra four hours per week, then, involves working faster and doing less. Try it; all you can lose is time.

Using Five Minutes of Time

"Do you have a minute," can also translate to a request for many more minutes of your time. It ranks right up there with the phrase "You're probably not going to want to hear this, but..." Realistically, you may not be able to do much with a spare minute, but you can become more effective using just five minutes of your time.

Grouping Work Into Categories

Use bits and pieces of time, and group related activities. Both of these are well-known time management maxims, but what do they really mean? Think about tasks in four ways: (1) Do they take the same concentration levels or mental gymnastics? Is this work that requires quiet time and a minimum of interruptions?

Group Similar Tasks

Second, do the tasks have a physical similarity, either in using equipment, or the place where the task is performed? For example, if you are using a calculator, then it saves time to tag on another small project that requires a calculator . If you're off to the photocopier, grab your folder labeled *To Be Copied*. (Make the folder fluorescent or neon colored, so you can find it on your desk.)

Group Common Procedures

Third, does the task take the same procedure, rules, format or action? If it's a task you do infrequently, then you might want to create your own checklist and staple it inside a folder. Think of it as writing your own job manual. If a task can be easily conceptualized into steps, then it can also be a candidate for being delegated or shared at some point.

The task may not be an easy one to do, even after breaking it into concrete steps, but sometimes, refreshing your mind about the procedure can act as a motivator and de-stressing agent.

Group Paperwork

The fourth commonality around tasks is whether the tasks take the same paperwork, forms, information, or personnel involved. Computers and word processors have started us all thinking like them: how can we adapt, change and modify to save writing and work for ourselves? Five minutes of your time, grouping the same type of work, can make a dent in your overall time use.

> ## Using Five Minutes of Time
>
> 1. Groups work into categories: similar concentration levels, mental work, or quiet time.
> 2. Group similar tasks: is the necessary equipment or location similar?
> 3. Group common procedures: use checklists, or create a procedure sheet or book.
> 4. Group paperwork: group invoices, forms, information, letters, may use similar formatting. Think like a computer: adapt, change, and modify.

Finding Extra Time

We are always searching for that elusive extra time: listen to yourself and others, as we promise we'll do something as soon as we have extra time. In a typical workday, when does that extra time appear? Every eight hours we spend at work we have about 480 minutes. Sometimes, minding 480 minutes is more like corralling a box of hyperactive, runaway gerbils. Like time, they scatter in so many directions at once, and you're lost if you blink too quickly! But time really has to be attended to in minutes. We need to pay attention to our minutes, because we can more readily control them.

Time Estimation

Most people underestimate time, rather than overestimate it. The quick trip to the bank, which should take ten minutes, drags into seventeen minutes at rush hour. The task at work gets an unexpected delay from another department. Add Murphy's Law, human nature, and a dash of bad luck, and you find yourself running two days late. Start by estimating tasks and projects before

Finding Extra Time

1. Estimate projects before you begin them. This creates a safeguard against underestimating a day's realistic schedule.

2. Look at repetitive, everyday tasks and try to streamline them. Read more efficiently, and tackle daily mail in a streamlined fashion.

3. Paper shuffling results in handling a piece of paper at least 10 times before action is taken. Make decisions and move your paperwork along.

you begin them. Every day, as you list your day's priorities, jot down a time estimate. Be mindful of what kind of time estimates you're running up. Is it realistic? Or, are you one of those optimistic souls who schedules 43 hours of tasks, say on Tuesday, and then become disgruntled when you haven't quite accomplished them by 2:00 PM.?

Detecting Extra Pockets of Time

Extra time is going to come from carving bits and pieces off regular and repetitive tasks, and by constantly fine-tuning them. Industrial engineers work on the premise that any procedure that is repeated frequently can be improved upon, and even slight changes may result in increased efficiency over time. Industrial engineers in factory settings do not expect workers to work consistency at peak efficiency; they factor in fatigue, boredom, and other performance issues. But yet, how many of us expect ourselves to function at 100% efficiency on all our tasks, every day?

Finding Shortcuts

Look at your everyday activities. Has habit made you inflexible as to shortening, adapting, or streamlining tasks? Watch how other people perform various tasks, and copy their timesaving steps. Time and motion steps divide jobs into smaller and smaller units of steps in order to find efficiency. If you can look at a steady log of your typical tasks, both estimated and actual time, then you can begin to discover shortcuts in common activities. For example, maybe you will find that reading work-related material with a high lighter, allows you to skim headlines and read more quickly. You might find that riffling your mail is habitual, but could be streamlined. Estimates are that 80% of all mail can be answered when read the first time. How much of your mail attains heirloom status because it doesn't get dealt with properly, in the first place?

Paper Tips

Remember the rule of paper shuffling: the average paper (and yours are undoubtedly, above average!) gets handled 10 times before you're finished with it! If you can carve off fifteen minutes a day in more effective paper migration, it results in a savings of five extra hours per month!

Keep time estimates, and concentrate on changing just a few of your regular, daily tasks to find your extra time. The minutes are adding up!

Time Pressure

"Many of us are in the state of timelock. Timelock is the condition that occurs when claims on our time have grown so demanding that we feel it's impossible to wring out one more second out of a crowded calendar," observes Ralph Keyes, author of *Timelock* (Ballantine Books, 1991). You only have to look around to notice rushaholics whirling by at breakneck speed, whether it's the pizza promised in less than 30 minutes, or the one hour photo developing. The pressure today is to do more in less time.

Amazingly, in a 1975 national Roper survey, most Americans believed they had about the right amount of leisure time. By the 1990s a majority admitted that they have less leisure time than ever before. Keyes' research indicated that 85% of his subjects felt they had virtually no "spare" time. What is the impact of this speeded up society and how does it affect you and your work? "How did life get so busy, it's pace so fast and furious?" asks Ralph Keyes.

Time Pressure

1. Take some of the pressure off your concept of time. The tighter you try to control time, the more it will allude you.
2. Try to manage time more in mind with your body's rhythms: use your peak energy times, and don't fill up every available minute with activities.
3. Cut down on incoming time stimuli: television, noise, required reading. Turn to low tech hobbies that engage your brain and hands.

Looking At Time Differently

Some strategies to ease the pressure of time: re-invent your concept of time, manage time organically, and seek sanctuary from time. Re-inventing your concept of time, means that you need to look at your attitude: are you engaging in a constant time battle with time as the encroaching enemy? Time can't be controlled, so your only recourse is to approach time in a more relaxed way.

Keep in mind that stress is the biggest obstacle to time; stress symptoms actually hinder you from being at your productive best.

Managing Your Body Clock

Managing your time organically, Keyes points out, is a way to move beyond the usual tactics of making lists, prioritizing those lists, checking them twice, and so on. You may work more productively by paying attention to your body clock. Remember that your body fluctuates with the season, sunlight, mood, age, work schedules, and all the other factors that can alter your internal body clock. "Take advantage of peak periods in scheduling your work; alternate head work with hand work." And this is imperative: don't make use of every moment; according to Keyes, this only increases tension while reducing effectiveness. "Remember," he says, "trying to get more done in less time usually results in rushed, stressful, sloppy work."

Time Sanctuary

Seeking sanctuary from time helps cut down on the overload of time consciousness. "One way to make time less hectic is to limit data input while seeking regular opportunities to ignore time altogether," claims Keyes. Turn off the TV if you use it as a backdrop to other activities; it's just noise congestion, and makes you feel overloaded. Don't wear a watch for a day; cover your clocks. Cut down on your incoming reading; pay better attention to fewer pieces: quality over quantity. Cultivate hobbies that become time-free activities, such as chess, quilt making, or fly-tying. The idea is to chose a hobby or activity that does not have built-in deadlines. Before you sign on for additional technology, such as a fax or modem, extra phone lines, or a beeper, ask yourself if you are making yourself even more accessible? Do you need a hassle-free zone?

The pressures of timelock will probably always be with us, and will invariably increase, instead of decline. The key to coping with clock shock is a personal commitment, one that can lead to grabbing back the control of life's tempo.

Jumpstarting Your Day

Jumpstart your own effectiveness with these strategies to finish blocks of work. Do something about interruptions. Closet yourself away, turn on a phone machine, beg, borrow or bribe someone into trading "phone-free" time, put a quarantine sign on your door, and bear traps on visitor's chairs. Don't interrupt yourself either: even if you have a blinding, brilliant idea about something else, write it down, and get back to the work at hand.

Group Related Tasks

Second, corral work into blocks. Use the classic time management strategy of grouping related items. A task may only take five to fifteen minutes, but it may be a high concentration one, requiring writing and mental effort. Piggyback another high concentration task onto the first one. Group items that all take the same equipment, computer, calculator, copier, dictating paraphernalia, and so on, and make them a block of work.

Using Time Estimates

Keep to your schedule and check off items you finish. If you really want to monitor your progress, keep time estimates of how long the work actually took; months later you can check the time estimates for timing on similar projects.

Recognizing Results

Don't let your work just keep churning out without some recognition on your part, that you've finishing chunks of projects, delegated work, or made significant headway into leftover projects. If you don't keep track of such work, you'll have no feeling of accomplishment; you need to see some progress, and you need to reward yourself for making it!

Gaining More Realistic Time Slots

Blocking out activities throughout the day stops you from committing the cardinal sin of time management, scheduling, say, 91 hours of work for a single work day. Everyone does it, at times, but it then becomes profoundly depressing when you can't seem to shoehorn tasks into the available time. By scheduling work projects in actual time slots, you cut back on unrealistic time allotment, and force yourself to analyze whether four hours spent on a task is truly worth your time. These strategies can give you a realistic jump on effectiveness and productivity, as well as a guideline toward where your time efforts are being spent.

Jumpstarting Your Day

1. Do something pro-active about interruptions. Stay on task, and don't interrupt yourself, either.
2. Group related items, and piggy-back tasks: high concentration ones with other concentration intensive ones.
3. Keep time estimates, and match finished work against the estimates.
4. Celebrate finishing portions of your work. For ongoing projects, that have many steps, note your progress on a daily calendar; keeping track helps you to see results and stay motivated.
5. Block out work time, and see if your scheduling matches the work priority.

Taking the Time for Detail

Do details drive you crazy? You may be detail phobic. People who are impatient with essential details thrive on planning and often have the ability to visualize a broad picture of how things can operate; but their downfall is that they often get bogged down on exactly who and how things will operate. "Don't worry," they often say, "we'll work out the bugs." Knowing their love for detail, you worry.

Getting Bogged Down With Detail

Managing time with an aversion to detail is not an impossible task, but rather a creative one. Detail wary individuals get caught up with a multitude of tasks that never get translated into routine tasks; they are often too impatient to handle follow-up. As a result, crucial tasks invariably fall between the cracks. If you have this tendency, appoint a watchdog (a colleague or family member) to say "stop" and force you at least to see what's involved in follow-up procedures on a task.

Follow-up Tactics

Secondly, arrange for follow-up procedures by making a To Do list that clearly assigns tasks, either to yourself or to others. Create simple paperwork systems to organize the information you need to track; it may keep tasks from entering the Land of the Lost. Typically, items get buried or forgotten, and the detail-phobic soul is most susceptible to overlooking items they should note. Made to order checklists are probably the most helpful guideline to utilize; it may take some initial time to create them, but the payoff will be that they keep you from being scattered and forgetful.

Using Ticker Files

Another helpful filing system is using a 31 day tickler files. Tickler files are 31 manila file folders, with 12 files labeled with the months of the year. Tickler files enable you to place reminders for various days, and stash important papers that are current. A tickler file keeps you automatically on top of troublesome dates like birthdays and anniversaries. Of course, one has to look at a tickler file on a regular basis for this system to be effective.

Detail Aversive?

1. Appoint a watch-dog: a trusted colleague, friend, or relative, to point out details that need to be nurtured.
2. Figure out a To Do List that clearly assigns tasks and follow-up (by you or others).
3. Use pre-printed checklists (of your devising) to track possessions, progress, and details.
4. Use a 31 day tickler file system, and check it everyday!
5. Carry index cards to make quick notes. Use a cassette recorder or personal organizer to record reminders.

Remembering Odds and Ends

Minimize your amnesia for details by recording your thoughts and ideas, either by always carrying index cards for fast jotting, or by using a portable tape recorder to flesh out more expansive ideas. Some individuals swear by the electronic personal organizers that can interact with your desk-bound computer. Tack up reminders for yourself in prominent places. Yes, your home and work place will look as if you won a five- year supply of adhesive notes, but overlook the jeers and comments of others. Detail can be conquered! It just takes some ingenuity to keep detail from overwhelming your time.

Interruption Time

Ask anyone why they can't manage their time, and they will invariably blame others for time shortages. It's those interruptions, the telephone that never takes a break, the insistent boss, and those equally insensitive co-workers. It may be the clients, the customers, the patients, or the students, but to whomever you attribute your time shortfall, it is usually someone else that eats up your time. It seems that everyone dreams of being left alone to get their work done. Is there something wrong in this equation?

The Myth of Interruption-Free Jobs

Granted, the majority of workers can churn out work when left undisturbed, without interruption. Some organizations even institute a "quiet time", when switchboards are shut down, visitors are not allowed, and co-workers purposely do not interact for an hour or two. Obviously, this strategy cannot work in all industries. But back to the concept of undisturbed time: most individuals have little idea of how they really spend their working hours. For example, look at the pattern of interruptions that plague your soul: are these regular interruptions that occur in a somewhat consistent pattern? Interruptions may involve the junior members of the staff, looking for decisions on procedure or policy. It could be other departments either reminding, or demanding that deadlines be met. Or perhaps it's those pesky customers with typical questions. (If only they'd stop bothering your company with their demands for service . . . !)

Re-thinking Interruptions

Another way to view those interruptions is, that those interruptions may constitute the pattern of your regular work: those activities, while they may be boring, tedious and repetitive, may be regular tasks that need to be integrated into your conception of time. Granted all interruptions are not regular and consistent, but in looking for the pattern, certain similarities emerge.

Tracking Interruptions

Try keeping track of interruptions for a week or two. How many interruptions can be attributed to policy? For example, someone has to interpret or explain procedures, or rules to a caller or visitor. It may signal that efforts are needed to "educate" or train your customer base in some other way. If the consistent interruption comes internally, from staff members, then there may be a need for cross-training, interde-

Interruption Time

1. Keep track of your interruptions. Are these regularly occurring interruptions that signal a lack of information, training, or procedure on the part of other people? Strategies may need to be created to counteract these regular interruptions.

2. Fifty to seventy-five percent of your regular workload will be routine work. Workers often only want to allot ten to twenty percent of their work time to regular work, and consider anything above that as interruptions.

3. Schedule regular and routine work, and leave about twenty percent of your time for typical interruptions.

partmental meetings, or simply a regular forum to share common issues. Companies who form interdisciplinary teams which cross-pollinate with staff from interconnected departments often find their communication problems drop dramatically.

Routine Work or Interruptions?

Interruptions may not be truly interruptions; they may simply be your routine and regular work. Most time budgets of managerial and professional workers allot ten to twenty percent of time to routine work. For regular work, the tasks that make up the heart of your job, constitute anywhere from 50 to 75% of your time. To gain control of your workday, you need to be able to schedule your routine and regular work, and have a firm sense of whether you are on target in getting your fixed work accomplished. Interruptions may not be whisked away with a magician's wand, but diagnosing them accurately is one step toward controlling them. It may help to remember the comments of the late Malcolm Forbes: "If you have a job without aggravations, you don't have a job."

Three Major Time Robbers

The great French writer Balzac had a remedy for making himself work at his writing. Stripping off all his clothes, he would give them to a servant and instruct him to lock his door until he was through with his task. This technique probably wouldn't work well in the modern workplace: there's probably some stuffy law. The idea, however, of isolating oneself has great appeal.

The Role of Time Interruptions

Like most people, you probably believe that interruptions keep you from being fully productive. It's estimated that if you time is out of control, and you're feeling that your accomplishments are meager, then, you're controlling only about 10% of your time. Ideally, you should be controlling about 50% of your time.

Most of us complain that we would be paragons of virtue, if only, just only, we could stop being interrupted by everyone around us. But the three major time robbers are actually: your personal time behavior, lack of planning, and third, interruptions.

Time Robber One: Personal Productivity

Your personal time behavior includes your personal productivity levels. Most people struggle with inner conflicts that lead to negative time use. For example, think of all the rationalizations that you can scare up for explaining why things don't get done. The dog looked a bit peaked last

Saturday; it was overcast, and so it probably wouldn't be a good day for cleaning, anyway. Only you can determine what is a optimum level of productivity for yourself. The question to ask is: are you under-employed on tasks, or over-employed? Are you really working at capacity level, and do you have a daily way to monitor this by checklists, daily planners, or to-do lists?

Three Major Time Robbers

1. Personal Productivity: how much you expect of your own performance is a critical indicator of how much you will accomplish. Do you have a process that monitors your accomplishments and goals?

2. Lack of Planning: determining exactly where you should focus your energies is the heart of planning. Stop being reactive to others priorities and distractions.

3. Interruptions: in a typical workplace you will be interrupted about every eight minutes; it takes approximately three to four minutes to regain concentration and get back on task. Focus your attention on springing back quickly from interruptions, and making decisions about your reactions.

Time Robber Two: Lack of Planning

The second major time waster is lack of planning. If we don't plan our days, the time slips away, and we may well berate ourselves later, for not accomplishing enough. Without planning, we become too reactive to everyone else's agenda, and at day's end, we find our work time has vanished, with little attention to our own priorities. Lack of planning also allows us to focus on the easy tasks, and procrastinate on the tougher ones.

Time Robber Three: Interruptions

The third major time wasters are the unnecessary interruptions that plague your life. Interruptions break concentration, and make it difficult to restart tasks. If you've been teetering on the brink of giving up on a task, then an interruption is often all you need to give up! Sometimes you can even help this process along, by working in areas where you can be physically interrupted. Interruptions then, are a definite problem in everyone's life, but not the major cause of most of our time mishaps. Go ahead, anyway: the next time someone interrupts you, blame them vigorously, and silently, of course. Who knows, you may have fueled enough adrenaline and vigor to complete your interrupted task.

Waiting Time

A recent survey ranked American cities on their time orientation. For example Kansas City ranks tenth among the "fastest" cities, with Buffalo ranking fastest and Los Angeles coming in last. These somewhat bizarre findings were calculated on a number of factors: how quickly people walked, how fast bank clerks and mail clerks completed transactions and questions, and the number of wristwatches worn by walkers. Does knowing this information help you quell your impatience when the drive-in lane at your bank is moving at sloth speed? Probably not.

Seven Years of Our Time

In these busy times it's helpful to give some thought to waiting. Time experts estimate that we spend seven years of our lives, waiting. (And you thought you were the only one to pick the longest lines!) Strategies to cut down on waiting time involve using off-hours, calling ahead, anticipating and planning, and expanding resources.

Peak Time Versus Our Time

Much of our most frustrating waiting time comes from peak times: getting gasoline on weekends, or before work, wand using bank or automated teller lines at lunch and just before closing. Some individuals find it helpful to designate one lunch hour per week as an errand wrap up day. It may not be your most stimulating lunch hour, but it may keep you out of the long lines.

You may find that your perfect cleaners, printers, or hair-cutter, have been discovered by too many other, resulting in slow service. Unless you're truly addicted to their service, you may save time by utilizing smaller establishments that are off the beaten path. Ask your suppliers about their slow times, and utilize those hours if possible.

Saving Your Time

Use your telephone to confirm all appointments, and confirm that work is finished. Glitches happen, and although you wont be thrilled about it, its better you spend your waiting time more productively.

Make certain you carry with you a small notebook and address book. You can write short notes or postcards, review shopping lists, or create new ones. Photocopying articles that you want to read and sticking them in your notebook will make you feel virtuous and prepared. We cant do away with all out waiting time, or demand of ourselves that we be produc-

> **Waiting Time**
>
> 1. You spend seven years of your time waiting!
> 2. Use off-hours, call ahead, anticipate and plan.
> 3. Consider changing services if your service providers have become too popular; use their slow times to do business with them.
> 4. Be prepared with some busy work (reading articles, and notebooks for lists) for the times you do have to wait.

tive every moment of the day. Benjamin Franklin warned us in his autobiography that "A perfect Character might be

attended with the Inconvenience of being envied and hated."
Don't be too good!

Memory Time

Writer Alexander Chase once observed that "memory is the thing you forget with." How many of us wander into another room and completely forget why we're there? It's not time to have your brain cells vacuumed, but perhaps some memory work is in order. Memory, scientists, tell us, is like a muscle. It weakens when it's not used, and builds and strengthens through constant use. Obviously, forgetting things gets you into a myriad of time troubles. What exactly do you have to remember?

Memory Power or Written Lists?

Discriminate what can be written down and what needs to be stored in memory. Individuals with hectic schedules and poor memories need to write everything down, even if they have to schedule forced memory sessions where they focus on exactly what they should be noting. Individuals who experience slippage with tasks need a memory list that is numbered; Aunt Berta's birthday makes the list as well as the preparation of quarterly reports at work, and then, both tasks get transferred to a calendar or To-Do list. The lists, of course, also have to be reviewed frequently.

Optimum Memory Time

Morning is the best memory time for most individuals, between 8:00 and 10:00 AM, as your brain is receiving fewer stimulus overloads. According to many memory experts, efficiency and memory powers drop off appreciably as the day lengthens. If you've noticed late in the day that your brain power most clearly approximates succotash, you're scientifically correct. Retentive powers loss strength and potency throughout the day, and by late afternoon your concentration measures approximately 6 to 10 percent less than earlier in the day.

> ## Memory Time
>
> 1. The busier you are, the more likely it will be that you write memory lists of tasks to remember. Transfer to daily To-Do lists.
> 2. Morning is the best memory time.
> 3. Use routine, and repetition of tasks to make everyday tasks automatic.
> 4. Add novelty to the task (creating a rhyme about it) to add impact to your recollection.
> 5. Actively visualize what you want to recall. Concentrate and get a visual picture of it.
> 6. Fatigue, illness, and prescription drugs will affect memory.

Memory Enhancers

To improve your memory, practice these four strategies. First, use mindless organization tricks. When you remove your shoes, put them in the same place; likewise, your car keys can be parked in a tray or basket by the door. Scissors and tape get returned to their storage place. It might take some discipline to return these items, but the payoff is that you cut down on retrieval missions. When you're abstracted or foggy, chances are, the car keys will not end up on the refrigerator shelf, but rather in their own little niche. Look around stationery stores and discount stores for organizers that fit your needs. If you keep travel receipts in the car, a mini-clipboard might keep them corralled more easily than stuffed in the glove box.

Memory Jolts

Second, jolt your memory with something different. If you regularly fog on tasks, such as whether you've locked your front door, add a novel way of completing the task. Make up a riddle about locks as you lock the door; an hour later, when you scour your memory, you'll probably remember the silly riddle.

Use Visual Imagery

Third, get a visual picture of what you want to remember. As you're introduced to someone, picture their name flashed on a giant scoreboard. Repeat their name and try to use it again in the next few seconds.

The Body/Mind Connection

Fourth, your body state influences memory. Fatigue will impair memory as well as common prescription drugs such as cold and allergy medicines, antihistamines, and pain killers.

80/20 Principle

You need to pick the vital ingredients. Sounds like a cooking lesson? No, it's simply a classic time management adage. The Pareto Principle, formulated by Italian economist Vilfredo Pareto, insists that 20% of the causes bring 80% of the results. For example, in decision-making we often wait for more facts in order to decide, but the reality is, that only 20% of the total facts involved are critical to 80% of the outcome. An example closer to home might be buying a gift for someone. We procrastinate, and wait until the eleventh hour, hoping that we'll get more insight, inspiration, or ideas for the perfect gift. The reality is, we often end up buying a gift that reflects the 20% information that we already know about that individual. Putting off gift buying often does not improve the eventual outcome – the gift. In fact, desperation can convince us that our recipient really wants that book on weasel migration patterns.

Focusing On Results

Picking the vital ingredients in any task forces us to focus on the outcome. What is crucial to make this task a success? What can we throw out as nonessential? By focusing on the outcome, where can we streamline the task?

Look at your projects for the coming week. Where do 20% of your efforts need to be focused? If you're feeling overwhelmed, and stress symptoms are starting to signal, then it's critical that a portion of that 20% of effort be spent on planning and organizing. Allocate some time to downtime, hobbies, or other stress-reducing activities. It will definitely impact on your 80% of the outcome – you will have corralled your tasks into some order, made a plan for accomplishing them, and applied some first aid for potential stress.

Troubleshooting

If you are having trouble figuring out your 80/20 Pareto rule, look back to a recent project or event. What went wrong? Was your time distribution allotted in the right arenas, or, were you spending 80% of your time on trivial items?

The Pareto Principle In Action

Ask yourself the question: "If I solve this problem, does it impact on activities for the future?" For

> ## The 80/20 Principle
>
> 1. Twenty percent of the causes bring 80 percent of the results.
> 2. Focus on your outcome. What are the vital ingredients that will make it successful?
> 3. Learn from your mistakes. Is your time allocation on target – or wasted on trivial items?
> 4. Will problem solving today buy you time in the future? Twenty percent of your time can be invested for 80 percent of results, later.

example, cleaning up your workstation may be time-consuming, and you may assign it a low priority. The result, though, may impact on your work for months to come. Your workstation cleanup may be the vital ingredient that accounts for 80% of your success in completing your work.

CHAPTER 5

More Time Strategies

Time Detectives

Once again the Japanese have pioneered a new work strategy: instead of wondering how they're doing in the workplace, they hire detectives to find out by running background checks on themselves. According to Mari Yamaguchi, in a Associated Press report, private investigators conducted about 2,000 investigations in Tokyo in a one year period. Detectives ferret out their client's promotional prospects at a company, and try to wade through tatemae, the diplomatic words that mask honne, or real feelings.

Hiring A Time Detective

Picture what could happen if this would catch on in the States. You're puzzled as to why your time management skills don't seem to be effective; it's a mystery as to where your elusive time goes. You hire a Time Detective to investigate your time use, and report back to you. Of course, the detective, bases his analysis on classic time management strategies and compares your performance.

The Confidential Time Report

The following is from the detective's confidential report: Principle: Utilize a daily To-Do list. Subject dutifully creates list, then loses it. Spends next hour looking for list. Resorts to using backs of used envelopes for list; at week's end has 57 dog-eared lists.

Time Principle Two

Time Principle Two, the detective notes, is: Harness high

energy levels for high-priority tasks. Subject opens and reads junk mail as day's first activity, and straightens desk. (This may be productive, the investigator notes, as the average executive spends 11 minutes per day looking for lost desk items.) However, two hours later, subject dozes off while reading latest budget figures. Analysis: open junk mail at nap time.

Time Principle Three

Principle Three, the detective duly notes, is: Energize projects by spending small blocs of time on tasks to spur motivation; try for a minimum of 20 minutes per task. The subject seems to wander about the workplace looking for diversion; subject was sighted admiring a co-worker's 56 photos of his home sprinkler system.

> **Five Classic Time Principles:**
>
> 1. Utilize daily to-lists.
> 2. Harness high energy levels for high performance tasks.
> 3. Spend small blocks of time on tasks to spur motivation.
> 4. Group related activities; high concentration tasks with tasks that are similar.
> 5. Finish tasks fully.

Time Principle Four

Principle Four suggests grouping related activities; pairing high concentration work with several tasks that are similar. Detective notes that subject's only ability to group related activities revolves around proclivity to combine food with every task. Twinkies with monthly reports, nachos with meeting agenda, and coffee rings on most paperwork.

Time Principle Five

Principle Five, finishing tasks fully, seems to be impossible for this client. The investigator counted 27 projects in various stages of completion, and the client was adding more; subject seems to think work can be controlled by the copious posting of yellow adhesive notes on every available surface.

Final Analysis of Time Skills

Confidential Assessment of Time Management Skills: Subject works approximately three hours per day (national average is just below five hours).

Subject seems to be constantly busy but does not accomplish much; subject is extremely disorganized and manifests a chaotic work style. Subject breaks every time management rule and even creates innovative ways to waste time (e.g. all office erasers have been turned into weird looking dog creatures.) Subject's time usage is abysmal, but unfortunately no seems to notice, and subject's skills seem to be superior to other co-workers. Promotion prognosis: excellent. (End of report).

Controlling 50% of Your Time

What percentage of your time do you expect to control? Most individuals will respond with an estimate ranging from 75% to 100 %. According to most experts you can only expect to be able to control only 50% of your time daily. So it's imperative that time be earmarked for productive activities. The 50% estimate shoots a hole in the theory that good time managers are calling their own time shots a majority of the time. In a way, the statistic is somewhat reassuring; there's not really a Shangri-Lai of Time somewhere, where the anointed have control of their time schedules.

Time Decision Making

Some other pointers to keep your day on track, is to make decisions quickly, avoid over commitment, and increase the extent of your delegation. The first strategy, decision-making, can be a real time waster. During the course of a typical day, there are a great many small details that need decisions. When you're feeling overwhelmed, decision-making is just one more hassle, and you may lose time just deciding. Keep in mind that an occasional poor decision on something trivial probably won't cause much havoc. Decide and move on!

Avoiding Over Commitment

The second strategy of avoiding over commitment involves the realization that there will always be new demands placed on you that come out of the blue. Check your calendar, your priority list, and your intuitive feeling, and then decide if this new request needs to be added. Your appointment calendar doesn't have to be guarded like Fort Knox; maybe the new request will add fun or interest to your life.

Adding Delegation Skills

The third strategy involves stretching the limits of your delegation skills. Try to delegate one new task a week. If you don't have legions of faithful minions standing in line to respond to your latest delegation, think about bartering services, hiring out, cutting down on your involvement, sharing a task, or streamlining the job so it makes it easier to do!

Time Slippage

If you expect a 20% or more slippage in your time schedule, you're probably close to accurate. Perfection is a lofty goal, but it rarely occurs. Now, armed with your 50% estimate of your run-away day, combined with a 20% "slippage" rate, do you now feel more psychologically in control?

Controlling 50% of Your Time

1. You can realistically control about 50% of your time.
2. Make decisions quickly.
3. For new demands, check your intuition, priority list, and calendar.
4. Think about creative ways to delegate: barter, trade, minimize, or share a task.
5. Time slippage will account for about 20% of your time.

Bureaucrat Time

The story is told that in 1803 the British created a civil service job for a man to stand on the cliffs of Dover with a spyglass. He was supposed to ring a bell if he saw Napoleon sailing into the English shores. The job was abolished in 1945. You probably have your own story of the bureaucratic obstacles that block efficiency or service. It may be the nine phone calls you have to make, because no one in an organization can answer your particular question. It may be playing organizational "hot-potato": individuals won't take responsibility for a problem, so you're tossed onto the next player in line. Or, you may be encountering an unworkable, and unwieldy system, like needing seven executive signatures to obtain a yellow, legal pad from supply. Whatever the bureaucratic stumbling block, you can identify three components of the blockage: it's an incredible time-waster, and tremendously inefficient.

Secondly, the procedures are often amorphous, or they are carved in stone: "We have always done it this way." Third, the individuals involved in the bureaucratic red tape are either operating without a clue, or you swear they're taken a daily vow to obfuscate and confuse the situation. Organizational expert Muriel Solomon calls them "the comma counters." What tactical strategies can you use to change or modify bureaucracy?

Changing A System

To change any system, you begin by questioning purpose, underlying beliefs, assumptions, and goals. Naturally, you will run into resistance and negativity on the part of individuals who think the system is working quite well, thank you, and you simply don't understand the scope of the "real" problem. Or more precisely, if you would just follow the 527-step procedure, you wouldn't have these problems.

To Help Change Rigid Rules:

1. Involve the rule-makers and chief bureaucrats.
2. Provide a low-key atmosphere to discuss change: work retreats or idea sessions.
3. Allow for face-saving and involvement. Try to envision a win-win solution for both sides.
4. Stay flexible and be open to any shift or moderate change.

Shifting Your Focus

Put yourself in the comma counter's work chair. They are being stubborn about change, because they believe that company policies are to be followed, not questioned. While their beliefs may be dogmatic and unyielding, they fervently believe that more adherence to the rules is needed, not less. (Meanwhile, you and the rest of the organization are tearing out your collective hair in frustration.)

You need to get them involved some type of forum where they can envision some differences; it could be a small meeting with the concerned: a work retreat, or a futuristically oriented "possibilities" meeting. Ask someone neutral to facilitate, so that your mutual resentments will be a little dissipated.

The Bureaucrat's Mind Set

Remember that bureaucrats see themselves as organized, super-efficient, and walking rule books, or historians of the organization. Use this to your advantage. Ask them to draw up a history of the problem; although you may be gritting your molars, they will be more participatory in their expert status. You are looking to include them, not exclude them from the process, and exclusion is their greatest fear in the change process.

Do Your Homework

If your opponents are really dogmatic and controlling, you may have to seed the creative process, because their style may inhibit creativity in a brain-storming process. Gather examples or success stories from other companies, utilize hero stories from business books and magazines, or view training tapes. Set up the session to be an atmosphere that inhibits individuals from taking a win-lose position on their ideas. The goal is for everyone to be flexible, and loosen their stranglehold on their ideas. Keep in mind Benjamin Franklin's adage: "All mankind is divided into three classes: those who are immovable; those who are movable; and those who move."

Time Logs

It's the end of the work week, and you have that sinking feeling: you're hopelessly behind, and your priorities are a vague and foggy memory.

You've been busy, but what have you accomplished? A look at your daily To Do list may not give you the answers, in fact, you may feel suicidal, looking at all the tasks that are uncompleted.

Many time management experts concur that keeping a time log for three to five days helps you to evaluate your lost time. The typical reaction to this task is resistance. Logically, if you don't have time now, you reason, you'll lose even more time by writing a time log.

Utilizing Time Logs

By definition, a time log is a complete record of how we spend our time. You record activities and record your priorities, from important to trivial. Include interruptions, no matter how short. (Visualize a five minute interruption multiplied six times a day: a whopping thirty minutes that mysteriously vanishes!) At the end of your day, or early the next morning, record your observations, or comments on how you rate your time performance. You may find that a longer coffee break got you off to a slow start in the morning. Perhaps you have a tendency to save your high priority items for late afternoon, and then you run out of time and energy as the evening beckons.

A time log can simply be similar in format to your daily calendar, as long as it can account for all the minutes in your day. Develop a shorthand system for yourself such as "m" for memo, "c" for call and "cb" for call-back. Just be consistent about your jottings, so that analyzing your logs is not an exercise in code-breaking.

Give It A Week

If you are truly serious about gaining control over your time usage, then keep the logs for at least a week. Analyze your pitfalls, and then try some changes the following week. Try breaking a few habits at a time. Rearrange phone call returns, re-schedule tasks like mail perusal, and coffee breaks. Look at the time, or lack of time, you spend reading industry publications. Note the time spent socializing in the office. Look at tasks that you handled that should have been delegated, or tasks that have the potential for others to be trained to do. Are there tasks on the list that needed an immediate and resounding "no" from the onset, but somehow became unwelcome priorities for you?

There are no easy or glib answers on the best use of your limited time. A time log, used consistently, can at least pin-

> **Time Logs**
>
> 1. If you're baffled as to where your time goes, keep a time log for a week.
> 2. Look at your time use: are you maximizing your daily routine tasks at the best time for them? Are you utilizing your high priority time for important tasks?
> 3. Are you delegating the tasks that

point some problem areas, and point you in the direction of change.

The seventeenth century French essayist La Bryere observed that, "Those who make the worst use of their time are the first to complain of its brevity."

Getting Down To Work

Do you work with fictitious frontiers? They are defined as illusive barriers that individuals construct when they want to put off dealing with a project, or undesirable consequences, according to management consultant, Tom E. Jones (Breakaway Management, Worx Publishing, 1996). Fictitious frontiers, for example, could be the upcoming holidays. "We'll start after the holidays, since everything will be too hectic." Or, that's a project that needs to be done after tax season, or vacation time, or after school starts a new year, or after the baby stops teething. Fictitious frontiers are just that: they are seemingly rational reasons that postpone and lower the urgency, or expectations for a project. Are you busy constructing fictitious frontiers for your time management?

Looking For Readiness Signals

Think back to the last self-improvement goal you were contemplating starting. Did you immediately assign it to a fictitious frontier of time? Motivation experts tell us to watch for the "readiness" that signals when we are motivated to begin change; in fact, some Eastern philosophers believe that when we are ready to learn, a teacher will appear. Pay attention to your own psychological cues that you are ready to begin a big task.

Determining A Starting Time

There are some specific ways to approach a task that helps bring your deadline closer to a reality. First, determine a time to get started. Waiting until you get caught up on other work, is a probably a fictitious frontier, not an actual starting date that can be tied to a calendar notation.

Getting Down To Work

1. Before you begin a task, look for readiness signals. Pay attention to your own psychological cues.
2. Designate an actual starting signal; its too easy to procrastinate on starting a task.
3. Gather your tools, resources, and supplies. (Having them on hand helps to propel you into the task.)
4. Identify a work space for your project.
5. Set clear guidelines for your task progression.
6. Give yourself small rewards along the way to keep motivated.

Gathering Resources

Second, gather any supplies that you need to get started. Become overly suspicious of your own motives if you determine you need supplies that have to be flown in from far-off lands, for example, like handcrafted notepaper from Nepal. Your delaying tactics may be deviously creative, but they remain procrastinating ploys, just the same. Easing into a task is facilitated by having materials and supplies handy and accessible.

Finding A Work Space

Clear your Work space, as well, and designate a space for your project's requirements. Giving a project "shelf space" makes the task more realistic. Pick your favorite place to start with a task. For example, if your task is writing a speech, and you like to search for quotes to use, do that first. The enjoyable task may well carry you into involvement with the project.

Setting Explicit Guidelines

Fourth, set some clear guidelines about your task progression. Obviously, you're not going to break the speed barrier on tasks you loathe and detest. Set several realistic time segments that are doable and believable. Estimate your work pace — are you good for a thirty minute stretch of solid work? Can you carry your momentum and re-schedule a regular work date until the task is done?

Staying Motivated

Give yourself small rewards along the way: look for small luxuries you can give yourself. Create interim checklists or checkpoints step by step so you can keep your eyes on your ultimate goal. Cut down on distractions and when you work, give the task your full attention; concentrate and immerse yourself in the work. The payoff is that you create some solid work habits that get you in and out of a task.

Time Bites

Most of us hate to wait. Time urgency makes us view any delay as an affront to our finely honed time schedules. Our blood pressure rises as we deal with clerks who have mastered Advanced Paper-shuffling. When you speed through a fast-food drive-through, you remember the current twist on service: clerks now deliver your order to your car, after an interminable wait. Or, you find the person at the bank window in front of you is trying to cash a check with an expired Moldavian driver's license. It's enough to make you become a hermit. What can you do to use your time fragments more effectively?

Everyday Strategies

Consider using non-peak hours. Lunch hours may be obviously busy, but you can ask the particular business or service when their lull hours occur. Second, project ahead. Can you double up on errands? Can you consolidate some services into one-stop shopping? Question whether your service areas need to be near your home, or your work. Does your workplace allow deliveries of particular services, such as dry-cleaning and prescriptions? Don't forget that catalog orders, as well, save you time and gas.

Your Banking Habits

Do you short yourself on cash and running money, and then waste time racing about cashing checks or finding an elusive automatic teller machine? It may be a false sense of saving, if you simply aren't getting enough greenbacks to get you through the week. You may also find yourself using credit cards more, for essentials like gas and drug store items, if you don't plan your cash expenditures.

Using Time Fragments

Ask yourself what you can do during a five minute wait. You might list a short phone call, a mini-balance of your checkbook, or a review of your calendar, which certainly beats chewing your nails, and becoming stressed out over a wait. If you work with people who keep you cooling your heels, waiting for meeting start-ups, or appointments, turn your thinking around. A more positive revenge is to plan to get some work accomplished while you wait. You can't change their bad habits, but you can lower your irritation level and be efficient at the same time. (Sometimes, keeping people waiting is a power play; your efficient use of the wait counteracts their strategy, and takes the fun out of it!)

The Essential Time Query

It helps to step back from tasks and ask: is there is an easier way to accomplish this? Do we need to

Using Time Fragments:

1. Run errands during non-peak hours. Double up and plot out your running; use services that deliver, and use mail order, as well.
2. Plan for daily five-minute time fragments. Have a list of tasks you can complete in short time slots.
3. Ask yourself daily: Is there an easier way to accomplish this task?

use some time investment now to streamline the task for the future? For example, one hobbyist found that he was always forgetting some essential piece of gear at home. By making a photocopied checklist of all his supplies, he kept on track, and made his preparation time easier. He didn't have to second-guess himself either, on whether something was packed in the car. Try it yourself with a regular task that needs streamlining.

All of us are hoping somehow, to magically extend our twenty-four hours. Analyzing our everyday activities and time-wasters may be one way to find that time extension.

Time Habituation

The note read: I can't go on. "My To Do list is a hideous travesty of things I don't do; my desk looks like the aftermath of a nuclear testing site. My priorities are suspect, and my appointment book is a shambles." It's regrettably unresearched, but few people leave suicide notes because of their time management, although there are probably days when the prospect looks inviting.

Most veterans of time management workshops can tell you they should be using their calendar planners, reviewing their day and working smarter. Great epitaphs, but do they work? The biggest problem in time management is habituation. Habituation is the process where people have a lessening sensitivity to stimuli. Why is the 37th bite of rum raisin ice cream not as scintillating as the first few mouthfuls? We have habituated to the taste.

Habituation Tendencies

When we habituate to our surroundings, we fail to notice and respond to stimuli. The folks at 3M, the makers of the ever present sticky notes (now 300 varieties) report that people often photocopy materials with incriminating information still attached. "Fred, this customer is the loudmouthed jerk I warned you about!" Who hasn't habituated to the little yellow squares? If you use them as memory joggers, one day you simply will become blind to the messages they impart. Habituation strikes again.

Habituation also allows us to continue poor habits. We

may allow ourselves to be interrupted and may not consider any alternative options like re-scheduling, being unavailable for a determined time, or simply saying no. Interruptions get precedence because we are so used to them. One perplexed manager came hunting for staff members because they failed to interrupt him on schedule. He thought they had expired at their desks.

Research On Habits

Gary English, a Florida based management consultant who studied achievement (*Training and Development Journal,* January, 1989) noted that patterned and non productive behaviors occurs in situations when a person's efforts are not tied in clearly with success. In a study of baseball players, it was determined that some players have a predictable set of behaviors before pitching and hitting a ball, but not before catching one. Fielders, who have a high success ratio when they perform well, do not, English observed. Since many workers jobs involve at best an uncertain link between their efforts and the company's success, one would expect many people

Time Habituation

1. Habituation allows us not to pay attention to surroundings, stimuli, and cues.
2. With habituation, we operate at a comfort level and often don't seek new behavior, or time-enhancing alternatives.
3. Habituation often lulls us into performing tasks at less than optimum conditions: for example, when our concentration levels are poor, we do the task out of habit, rather than switching routine.

to indulge in some useless activities that can be identified and eliminated.

Habituation and Concentration

Habituation keeps us opening our mail at 10 a.m. when 10 a.m. may be the apex of our high concentration time, more suited to complex mental gymnastics like complex figures or detail. Instead, we're poring over the mail's latest promises of sweepstakes and office supply catalogs. Habituation has us tackling tough problems, when our energy level closely resembles that of iceberg lettuce. Better to shelve decision-making until our synapses are operating on all cylinders.

Habit and routine can aid us in getting the mechanics of our daily life in order, but can be deadly if the routine lessens our ability to find alternative ways of being more efficient. Mark Twain observed that "Habit is habit, and not to be flung out of the window by any man, but coaxed downstairs a step at at time."

Dog Days

July third marks an auspicious holiday. (No, it's not the ninth hour to scurry across state lines and buy illegal fireworks...) July third to August fifteenth marks the beginning of Dog Days, the hottest days of the year in the Northern Hemisphere. Dog Days were popularly believed to be an evil time when the sea boiled, wine turned sour, dogs grew mad, and all creatures became languid, causing man to burn fevers, hysterics and phrensies (from Brady's *Clavis Calendarium*, 1813).

The ancients were obviously describing the typical Midwestern summer. During the Dog Days our ancestors tried to appease the star Sirius by sacrificing a brown dog, since Sirius was thought to bring the hot, sultry weather.

Staying Productive

Since dog sacrifices are definitely out, how can you keep productive at work during the dog days, when otherwise prone to hysterics and phrensies? A recent study suggests that you don't have to work like a dog to be effective. Researchers are finding that having fun at work increases productivity. Investigators at the University of Maryland discovered that people who felt good after a humorous film solved problems more creatively. Likewise, people who see problems as games come up with more solutions than people who view their problems as work.

In *The Hundred Best Companies To Work For In America*, authors Levering, Moscovitz and Katz give many examples of playfulness and fun at work that occur in highly successful companies. The authors recommend laughter, jokes, and joy in general as essential tools of management for defusing tension, making meetings more productive, and heightening creativity.

Working Hard To Have Fun

Why is it sometimes so hard to view the workplace in a lighter vein? One theory is that having fun at work violates our Puritan work ethic, and matches the belief that fun equals lowered productivity. But workers who report having fun at work, according to a California survey, reported in *Psychology Today* (March 1989) are less absent, or late to work, meet work demands more effectively, and are more creative at work. They are also less depressed, and more satisfied with their jobs and their lives in general. All these characteristics don't prove that fun at work is responsible for creating the all-American worker. It does point out, however, that workers who enjoy their jobs suffer less boredom and conflict, which may lead to higher job performance.

Having Fun At Work

1. Make a conscious effort to have more fun. (Appoint a committee, plan some work activities that are lighthearted and joyful).
2. Companies can encourage supervisors and managers to have more fun; they can also approve of company-wide contests, campaigns, and activities.
3. Work rewards can also be lighthearted and fun; give awards and recognition for all types of work behavior.

Suggestions For Adding Fun

How can you have more fun at work, retain your job, and still be productive? It's not necessary to wear pig snouts or hunt up whoopee cushions. David Abramis, Ph.D., a leading researcher at California State University offers these suggestions. First, make a conscious effort to have fun. Set fun goals for yourself and your subordinates--such as attending company get-togethers more regularly and setting up challenges for yourself--just as you set more traditional goals of performance and accomplishment. You might even include having fun as a goal when you set performance standards. Next, help supervisors and other managers have fun and suggest ways they can help their people do the same. Odetics, a high tech robotics company in California has had a Fun Committee since 1982, and it sponsors Hula Hoop contests, bubblegum competitions and telephone booth stuffing.

Third, use rewards and recognition to let people know they are valued. The rewards don't have to be formal and bureaucratic, notes Abramis, they can be spontaneous and personal.

When the dog days of summer descend, have some fun, and stop working like a dog.

Remedial Time Management

Your boss has made very pointed comments about your time management. Your co-workers tell wonderful "corporate folk-tales" about your time management disasters. Your family sighs, and act as if they've become resigned to your personal foible. You don't want to appear paranoid, but is someone trying to tell you something important about your time management skills?

If you were signed up for Remedial Time Management 101, where would you focus? Would it be in enhancing your planning skills? Do your time management challenges come from jumping from project to project, and never quite finishing anything to your satisfaction? Is chronic lateness a problem? Do stress symptoms interfere with your time usage? Do you do all right with your day to day activities, but never touch your long term priorities? Some specific strategies are called for to streamline your time efforts.

Pick A Time Issue

First, isolate one particular time issue. We usually want instant change and instant results when we embark on any self-generated improvement. Think small and strategically: what incremental behavior change would give you the most in benefits? If you could move a behavior toward twenty percent more effectiveness, what impact would it have on your work? Make your goal very specific. A goal that is specific in detail as to outcome reduces confusion and clarifies what is expected of you. "Being better with time" is a lofty goal, but a useless one, because it is too abstract. "Finishing weekly reports by Thursday noon" is a specific goal.

Find A Way To Measure Your Goals

Second, a goal needs to be measurable in three concrete ways. It needs to identify the particular behavior involved. For example, arriving on time for Monday's staff meeting, identifies a particular behavior. Next, the goal needs a way to be quantified: an accurate way to measure behavior that doesn't rely on guessing to determine progress. To make a goal measurable, it needs a specific deadline. Exactly when are you planning your new "on time" behavior?

Remember the British saying: "Someday is not a day of the week."

Staying On Goal

To make your time management behavior stick, your original goal has to be challenging. If you make the task too easy, you lose interest; if it's too hard a task, you become discouraged and bogged down.

Remedial Time Management

1. Pick a time issue; think small and strategically: what change will give you the most impact on your work?
2. A goal needs to be: (1) identified in specific behavioral terms; (2) able to be accurately measured—counted, marked, etc.; and (3) needs a specific deadline.
3. Your goal has to be challenging—not too easy and not too difficult.
4. To make your goal stick you have to translate your goal into daily activities. Make a contract and re-remind yourself of your promised goals.

Making Your Goal Into A Routine

Lastly, for any behavior change to make significant affect on your time, you have to make the goal into a daily activity; you need to actively bring the goal into present focus rather than just wishful thinking. Write yourself a contract, promise yourself you'll scribble it down on the top of your everyday planner, or affix it to your car's dashboard, but get that goal out there so you can have a visual reminder of what you've pledged to do for your time.

Time Planning: 60/20 Ratio

If you ask anyone how much of their time they would like to control, most individuals will opt for 75 to 100% of their time. Unless you're a hermit sealed in a cave, you can probably only control 50 to 60% of your available time. One classic ratio in time management is the 60:40 rule. You need to visualize your working day in three blocks: approximately 60 percent of activities planned; approximately 20 percent of activities unplanned (reserve for buffers and unplanned activities), and approximately 20 percent for spontaneous activities, such as leadership tasks and creative periods.

Typical and Atypical Work Weeks

Look at the activities that make up your typical week. Although most of us decry that we have "typical" days, there is a startlingly consistent pattern to our time use. Chances are in a given week, you will fill up your car's tank, go to the store, straighten your work site, eat some meals in or out, and so on. What isn't typical is the 20 to 40 percent of your activities that come out of nowhere − the walk-in customer, the emergency, the opportunity that you can't pass up. If you are charting your time realistically, then planning for the unexpected is good planning. If you don't need your planned "unplanned" time then you have what the Creoles call a lagniappe, an unexpected gift. You can give the gift of time to yourself. Use the time for a breather, some play time, or simply to reward yourself for planning ahead and gaining free time. If you feel like being a good automaton you can plunge headlong into some serious work, and feel morally superior, at least until your next crisis.

Overwhelming To Do Lists

Make certain you don't over plan. Over planning can often be detected by the "To-Do" list that could double for a roll of wallpaper. There is simply no way the activities listed could be accomplished in one week. If you are constantly operating in a time deficit, then begin by estimating how long a task will take. Jot down your estimate, say two and hours for a client meeting and review.

After the meeting, compare the actual time. Continue this estimation and time watch of some of your major activities for the next week.

Time Estimation Results

This process allows you to plan how much time, ideally, you want to allot to certain tasks. This time estimation allows you to see potential time wasters, particularly for tasks that have a way of growing to fill the allotted time. For example, if you allow one hour for a lunch meeting, and the reality time check is closer to two, or two and a half hours, you've spotted a potential time robber that will throw off your planning. If you factor in these unconscious, longer long lunch hours a few times per week, you have uncovered a

Visualize Your Work Day As:

1. Sixty percent of your activities should be planned.
2. Twenty percent of time should be unplanned.
3. Twenty percent should be reserved for spontaneous activities or creative tasks.

huge time hole.

Since the time has to come from somewhere, you usually end up shorting other tasks, or worse, not even touching them. Your "To Do" list becomes a shambles, and you start the next day running behind. To get your time back on a more even keel, keep your time estimates for awhile, and get a firm sense of the amount of time your re-occurring tasks really take.

Making Time For Innovation

The French writer Andre Gide once observed, "One doesn't discover new lands without consenting to lose sight of the shore for a very long time." Business experts predict that organizations that will survive turbulent business upheavals will be those that are creative and innovative. Those companies who are doing "business as usual" will perish. Why are innovation and creativity so difficult to achieve?

One primary reason is that it takes time to change. Most people admit that they're lucky to get their jobs done, let alone be creative and visionary.

Barriers To Creativity

What gets in the way of our workplace creativity-- besides, piles of papers, overdue assignments, and unreturned message slips? The main barriers to creativity and innovation are rigid thinking and inflexible procedures. Scientists, who have studied creative individuals, found that the most creative were five-year-olds! Try telling a five-year-old that a giraffe can't be purple, or polka dotted, or plaid: you'll see creativity in action!

Many creativity experts believe that almost everyone is creative to some extent. Historically, many job classifications, such as blue collar workers or support staff were believed to be devoid of creative individuals; this, of course, is untrue. Creativity follows the individual, not the job title. Companies have often narrowed the avenues for creativity and innovation for certain jobs. So, for those seeking some creative solutions to old problems, the key question is: how does creativity become nurtured on the job?

Company Culture and Creativity

A company's atmosphere is one of the single, most important factors in determining the level of innovation and creativity, overall. In ideal circumstances, a company's atmosphere nurtures and encourages creative thought. If an employee comes up with an innovation, that person should be encouraged to develop the idea, and then the individual should be held accountable for the project. If the idea is not useful, or workable, the employee's efforts in trying to be creative, should be recognized. Employers should encourage them to continue thinking creatively, even if the idea cannot be implemented successfully. Remember that creativity also motivates and hooks employees into higher performance and productivity.

> **Nurturing Creativity in the Workplace**
>
> 1. Creativity is possible for all job titles and positions.
> 2. Companies need to provide recognition programs, bonuses, and rewards for creative ideas.
> 3. Creativity flourishes in organizations where senior management shares company vision, plans, and goals with the total organization.
> 4. Creativity is nurtured when management shares what is right with the organization, and what needs changing.

Encouraging Creative Thought

If your organization doesn't have a company-wide policy

of rewarding new ideas, then lobby for one, or begin on a smaller scale. Provide recognition for the person, despite their title. Many American corporations, particularly ones paying bonuses for ideas, find a surprising number of excellent products and marketing ideas come from individuals in a wide variety of job titles.

For maximum ideas, senior management should be added to the mix involved in the creative process. They should meet with various departments on a periodic basis to share company goals, discuss where the organization is going, what it is doing, and what it is doing wrong.

Managers can help nurture innovation and creativity by imparting the idea that in innovation, failure is not a sin. Alexander F. Osborn, American advertising executive, observed: "Creativity is so delicate a flower that praise tends to make it bloom, while discouragement often nips it in the bud. Any of us will put out more and better ideas if our efforts are appreciated."

Banking Time

Its a mob scene: Vans, cars, and buses all pull up to a store with a neon sign that reads: "Time For Sale." Once, inside, customers mull over the menu, and then shout their frantic time orders: "I need more hours". "Give me a side order of longer weekends," orders another. "Can I order an eight day week?" they beg.

The worst part is that if wiley entrepreneurs could figure how to package and sell time, there would be franchises galore with a steady stream of customers at time stores. Desperate time consumers would always be looking to find that extra and elusive hour. The bottom line for most individuals is that they're faced with the reality that the day can't be expanded to a more manageable 28 or 33 hour day. Instead, the extra hours have to come out of current activities, and time allotments.

Your Time Wish List

To start this process, make up a wish list of all the things you would like to do, but don't have the time. Be expansive, and dig out activities and interests you've dreamed about. Your wish list can include both work and leisure projects, as well as exercise or fitness programs. What would you read? What new skill would you learn if you had the time? Where would you travel? What other activities would you embark upon?

Think of your time as savings in a time bank. We all enjoy the same twenty four hours, but it is our pattern of allotting those hours that determines whether we are effective with our time.

Unless we are absolute time wizards, and we've conquered all our bad habits, and use our time at top efficiency – then we probably have room for improvement. Most time management experts believe that the average individual in general time usage, spends about 50 to 70% of their time and energy doing unimportant, nonworthwhile things in the least effective way. What areas of your time use are irrelevant and non-worthwhile? Most

Banking Time

1. Create a time wish list. Be fanciful: what would you really being doing if you had the time?
2. You are probably spending 50 to 70% of your time doing unimportant things in the least efficient way: your 50 to 30 % time is spent on your high priorities.
3. Look at two to three activities per day that you can streamline. Start saving your odd bits of time and devote them to items on your wish list or pet projects.

individuals can isolate some areas of their leisure time as candidates for activities that aren't worthwhile, such as camping in front of the TV, and getting hooked by the network's three hour program line-up. All of a sudden, it's the late news—and voila! The evening has vanished.

Trivial Work Goals

In deciding which work activities are irrelevant and not as worthwhile to your overall work goals, the task becomes more difficult. Isolating work activities that enhance your productivity is an easy measure: look to your level of planning, your skills at anticipation, your ability to manage fire-fighting, and keep crises at bay. View your track record of meeting your project deadlines, keeping current tasks completed, while finding time for higher level targeted accomplishments. For obvious time robbers look at office socializing, day-dreaming, a heavy preponderance of low-level clerical tasks, failure to delegate, procrastination, or perfectionism, and general disorganization.

Streamlining Strategies

Look to small bites or segments of your day to streamline. Is there one activity that you could modify, shape, or adapt? Working on one segment of your time behavior may not seem like tremendous progress, but it's those bits and pieces of time that add up over a week's time. Start saving your odd bits of time, and invest them in some long-term yield returns in your pet projects. The franchises for drive-up time stores may be a long time coming.

CHAPTER 6

Coping With Other People: Maximizing Your Time Use

Five Deadly Sins of Time Management

Managers can fall into some poor time management habits that impact on their own employees. Worse, managers will probably never get clued into these bad habits, since employees usually don't critique their boss's performance, at least, not within their hearing. If some of these traits sound embarrassing familiar, it may be wise to make some time management changes.

Bad Habit: Number One

The first bad habit is procrastination. Sure, we all do it, but if employees are actively nagging a boss about a work issue or problem, or overtly complaining, then it's time to re-evaluate your procrastination ploys.

Bad Habit: Number Two

The second habit is operating on "boss time," which has as its underlying principle, that "boss time" is valuable, expensive, and important, and employee time is not. Bosses may play out this behavior by coming to their own meetings late, allowing employee conferences to be interrupted constantly, and by giving employees the consistent message that everyone else comes first.

Bad Habit: Number Three

The third bad habit that managers can fall prey to, is not giving an employee autonomy over their own work space. Work styles vary enormously; a savvy manager will allow for individual differences that don't compromise workplace standards. For example, one manager objected to a "To-Do" list

posted on a cubicle's bulletin board. Although, the
list was visible in a public
area used by customers, the
puzzled employee inter-
preted it as a case of managerial muscle flexing. The
manager believed that by
teaching the employee to
keep the list on a desk, he
was modeling a better, and
more organized time strategy. Since he was the man-
ager, he reasoned, he knew more efficient techniques.

> ## Five Deadly Sins of Time Management
>
> 1. Procrastination.
> 2. Operating on boss time (Your time is more valuable than underling's time).
> 3. Failing to give employees freedom and autonomy toward their personal work space.
> 4. Taking too much time to solve employee's problems.
> 5. Keeping deadlines a surprise.

Bad Habit: Number Four

Taking too much time to solve employee's concerns is the
fourth bad habit. By the time employees have bearded a manager about a problem, they are probably fairly frustrated; they
have already tried to work it out, or at least, have suffered
some stress reactions over it. If managers drag their feet
about problem-solving, the problem may eventually solve
itself, but employees, like pachyderms, have long memories.
They will harbor resentment about the time delay, long after
the problem is gone.

Bad Habit: Number Five

Keeping deadlines a surprise is the fifth bad habit. Some
managers, when asked to implement changes that may be

unwelcome, will keep quiet about them, springing them at the last minute. Surprise attacks, even in warfare, are not considered polite. In reality, many employees possess topnotch information gathering skills that equal spy training, and probably already know about the changes. They are simply waiting the boss out.

These bad habits are easy ones to fall into; look at your own behavior, and see if you're ensnared in any time management traps.

Time Drains

In the comic strip "Li'l Abner," one of the classic characters was Joe Btfspik, who traveled through life with a permanent black cloud over his head; he was always in the wake of disasters, earthquakes, and other calamities. People ran when he came into sight. Do you have a covey of Joe Btfspiks at your workplace? They can be recognized by their gloom and doom predictions about work and life in general. They complain constantly about issues at work, and are the first to spread the latest discouraging word. They also tend to eat up pockets of your time, because complaining about the company invokes minute detailing of the latest rumors and downturns.

Disease Diagnosis: Chronic Complaining

This behavior is chronic complaining, and it is contagious! The complainer dumps their problems on first one person and then the next. The problems get worse with every re-telling, and there is a contagious aspect. Each person then plays "Can you top this?" with horror stories of their own. The result is a heavy dose of pessimism, depression and fatigue in the workplace. (It goes without saying that chronic complaining can be continued in your spare time at home!) To be fair, griping about work has always been close to an Olympic category by itself. Certainly, some grousing and griping allows us to blow off steam, and then scurry back to our cubbyholes to dig in for more work. When does it become a problem? Most stress experts agree chronic complaining is potentially harmful when it becomes habitual, and

Time Drains

1. Chronic complaining increases your pessimism, depression, and fatigue in the workplace.
2. Learn to express negative emotions in a positive way: problem-solve, or re-frame your complains with humor.
3. Seek out positive people and surround yourself with their upbeat attitudes.
4. Tell co-workers you're trying to work on not complaining about your job; it might lessen their chronic complaining.

individuals avoid looking to themselves for the causes and solutions to their problems. Entire organizations can get into the blame game, shifting blame from unit to department to branch. Employees soon learn to cast about lest they be caught in the witch-hunt of blame.

Boundaries for Complaining

To avoid chronic complaining, the key is to learn to express your negative feelings in a positive way. You may need to ventilate, but set some boundaries for yourself. Does re-enacting the work stress simply raise your blood pressure and anger levels again? You may be cycling yourself right back into a repeat of all your original emotions. Instead, see if you can recount your experiences in a funny or dramatic way. Comedians exaggerate and use absurdity to make us laugh. Can you do the same thing with your complaints?

Staying Positive

Try to gather positive people around you; zero in on their ability to remain energized, proactive and upbeat. When ventilating about your problems, balance it with some positive energy gain, such as some quiet time, allowing yourself a coffee break, a brisk walk, or simply, a reflection of the positives of the situation.

Tell co-workers that you want to break "your" habit of daily complaints, and ask them to encourage you when you're falling back into pessimism and gloom. Chances are, they will see the effect of some of their own behavior.

Beat the Joe Btfspiks at their own sport!

Being Late

Oscar Wilde created a character who commented wryly that "Punctuality was the thief of time." All of us run late at times, and as the rule dictates, the unexpected is bound to happen, when you don't have a nanosecond to spare. Perhaps lateness is not your problem, but rather, waiting for others seems to eat up your time. How does others' lateness impact on your time management? How often do meetings run over, because your colleagues are fifteen to twenty minutes late? How often do you cool your heels waiting for other's deadlines? If you run reasonably on time yourself, late behavior is guaranteed to drive you to strong addictions.

The Impact of Lateness

Review the cast of characters in your life, and you'll find invariably, that the same culprits are eternally late. It may even be the case for your own boss. Proper boss etiquette dictates that you don't reciprocate in kind, by also being late. The very day, you rationalize being twelve minutes late for a boss-dictated meeting is, of course, the only day that year, that your boss is running on time.

Many bosses, who treat employees like the office furniture, (it's just sitting there anyway, doing nothing) and don't respect their employee's time, are giving their underlings mixed messages, to say the least. The message is a jumbled metaphor of tired business axioms, like time is money, rank has its privileges, and a boss never wastes an employee's time because the employee's time is the boss's time, or, some convoluted logic similar to that. In reality, it works something like this: if time is, indeed a power tool, and those who hold power are allowed to waste the time of the less powerful, then that attitude will eventually permeate the entire organization. Co-workers, following their boss's example, will allow themselves to be less diligent about their time, dead-lines and promises to other co-workers, who they have designated as being less powerful or important. The result of course, is workplace anarchy, or failing that, grumpy co-workers and immeasurable time lost.

Being Late

1. If you analyze who is constantly late in your life, it will probably be a narrow range of friends, family, and co-workers.
2. If your boss keeps you continually waiting, don't reciprocate by being late in turn: your boss still has performance appraisal power over you.
3. Don't mimic a boss's late deadlines with your co-workers; it's still late behavior.

Reacting to Late Behavior

Savvy work behavior commands that you don't permit the poor work habits of a boss to influence your time manners. You may not be able to control other's behaviors, but you can treat others' time as you would like yours to be treated.

Time and Job Performance

What does it take to be successful in your job in the current business climate? Showing up for work is a good start, but there are actually three key factors in job performance.

Strategy One: Create A Professional Image

First, create a professional and credible image; secondly, deliver better work than expected, and third, leverage your performance. It isn't enough to simply perform your job, you have to self-manage your career, as well. To create an image of professionalism you need to treat your image — indeed your whole career—as a public relations project that you are managing and marketing.

Strategy Two: Delivering Premier Work

Delivering better work than is expected involves both time management and quality. A recent Accountemps study indicated that top managers knew more than their subordinates about business news, and more about local, national, international news, while middle managers were more up on sports! What is your business IQ?

Obviously, gaining control of information and reading is a skill for upward career progression. Being able to access key reports and figures in a meaningful way gives you an extra career edge.

Strategy Three: Getting Noticed

To maximize your performance, look for the projects and jobs that will bring your efforts to the notice of your superiors.

Projects should be chosen that will add results, profits, recognition, quality, or increased productivity to your organization.

Strategy Four: Insisting on Professionalism

It isn't enough that you carefully chose your work projects carefully; you need to expand your definition of quality and professionalism. Quality should not be relegated only to the outcome of a finished product, but should be a reflection of your professionalism in all areas of your job. In other words, no task is too small to be less than high quality. Keep your eyes open, and be willing to perform trouble-shooting tasks, especially in areas where other people won't bother to do so. You'll gain valuable perspective with trouble-shooting tasks.

Strategy Five: Small Things Add Up

Don't overlook small details that impact on your professional image. For example, don't let your name be attached to hasty, misspelled memos, e-mail, or letters. You may not be directly responsible for sloppiness, but it's a detail that conveys a lack of quality control on your part. If it has to carry a message about your performance take the time to make it right!

> **Time and Job Performance**
>
> 1. Create a professional and credible image.
> 2. Deliver better work than is expected.
> 3. Leverage your job performance, and allow work projects to show off your expertise and professionalism.
> 4. Self-manage your own career. Think of yourself as your own public relations client.

Criticism and Job Performance

When Deborah Bright was ranked one of the ten best American women divers, she didn't mind when her coach would relentlessly criticize her. Even under a harsh barrage of criticism, she stayed attuned to what he was saying about her performance. Years later, Bright became an educator and consultant to organizations, and she remembered the relationship with her coach. Interviewing other athletes as well, Bright concluded that the coaching relationship was somewhat unique. Both coach and athlete are concerned with performance, and the motivation behind criticizing the performance is a positive one; criticism is honest and is geared toward wiping out poor habits.

But why does most criticism in the workplace have exactly the opposite effect? Criticism more often results in resentment, and often ends up negatively affecting relationships. Criticism also impacts on time management, because criticism is often a factor in both procrastination and perfectionism.

In *Criticism in Your Life* (MasterMedia, New York, 1988), Deborah Bright researched the area of criticism, and developed some interesting techniques to view criticism as a positive force, one that enhances your performance and growth.

Criticism about our integrity hurts the most. Our stress levels zoom when our integrity level is being questioned. The most frequent criticisms come from bosses and mates, who often criticize when they're tired and cranky. (Warm milk and graham crackers may be order.) If you automatically "personalize" criticism, then you are failing to filter out what may be inaccurate or overblown. Personalization also serves to anchor the criticism with us, despite the accuracy or inaccuracy of the actual criticism. The criticism may be absolutely untrue, but personalizing it makes it real to our self-esteem. Gender studies have indicated that women often personalize and integrate criticism and blame, whereas males tend to blame others and situations, rather than integrating the criticism personally. Whatever your style, the antidote to personalizing criticism is to check it out with someone you trust, then decide if the criticism is valid and needs to be acted upon.

If you are the critic, you've heard the oft-quoted "sandwich method" of inserting the criticism between two pieces of praise. Detractors often claim the "sandwich technique" would only distract a kindergartner. You do need to use praise as a balance, because people who only use criticism run the risk of losing credibility. It can be an easy habit to focus on only the negative aspects of other people's behavior; but then, any future criticism can be written off as proof of being an incurable wet-blanket. Know what you want before delivering criticism, and know the type of action the receiver needs to take. If you cannot identify a specific action, you may want to delay giving the criticism for awhile.

If you feel the need to vent and rage before you begin criticizing someone else, then cooling off is definitely in order, so your criticism can be tempered by logic and not emotion.

Understanding criticism, and developing the skills to manage criticism fosters a personal sense of empowerment that lowers stress, and helps in regaining a sense of control.

Your ability to weather criticism is a valuable personal characteristic that can help you immeasurably on the job.

Saying No

American humorist Alexander Woolcott once observed: "Many of us spend half our time wishing for things we could have if we didn't spend half our time wishing." Do you often wish you could say "no"? How many times do you say "yes" to requests because you feel obligated? You say "yes" because you don't want to appear negative? You say "yes" because it seems too complicated to say "no"? You say "yes" even though the request will put you into a time bind. You say "yes" because to say "no" seems unkind and unreasonable.

Such is the complexity of our decision-making process. Psychologist Joseph Zinker noted that, "Only after you give yourself the permission to say "no" can you say "yes" and genuinely mean it."

Demands on your time, energy or resources are a critical factor in effective time management. You may manage your time well except for the area of requests from others. How do you calculate the correct ratio of "yes" versus "no"?

By this time, we think logically, everyone in the Western Hemisphere has mastered the art of saying "no". Many experts on assertive behavior point out that even very assertive souls become tripped up by requests. Look back on last month's activities. Did your time reflect a balanced blend of work and leisure time? If it didn't, what activities got in the way? Did requests for your time tip the balance?

The first step when presented with a request is to evaluate it. How does it fit in with your overall time goals? Does it add meaning and value? Or, is the activity one you'll do out of friendship, affection, or sense of community? More importantly, does the activity thrust you into a time conflict with your current responsibilities?

Second, realize that many requests take time to evaluate. When you are rushed or pressured, you react like a cornered squirrel and promise anything to get out of the situation. When remorse and recrimination set in later, you'll berate yourself for your momentary lapse of sanity.

Third, ask yourself if this is a request that needs some conditional limits set for it. "Yes," you valiantly promise, "I'll car pool the hyperactive, squirming soccer players, but only for the first four games, not for the entire season." You may want to use your evaluation time to set up definite limits to avoid over-commitment. Don't be afraid to design ground-rules; it helps define your responsibilities and clarifies for your requester, what you're willing to do, and not do.

Lastly, if your requester is adamant and persistent, or even whiny, demanding and manipulative, don't be afraid to negotiate. Career strategist Adele Scheele, Ph.D., once wrote that the beginning of successful career management is to recognize that "this is a negotiated world." Assess the request and identify the requester's priorities, as well as your own. To emphasize both your viewpoints you might say: "You want," and "I need....". Hammer out a compromise that you can honor. Re-check your priorities and time budget.

Remember that one of the tools in keeping your time in

check is to be diligent about limits. You may need to restate your limits again and again to people who are pushing your boundaries. It doesn't mean your vertebrae is made of jelly, but rather, that you need persistence to keep your limits intact. In business relationships, it also helps to keep a written record, memo, or notes so you can remind the other person about your previous agreements. Don't feel undermined or discouraged when others push your limits: it's simply human nature to ask for more. Didn't poet Robert Browning observe that "a man's reach must exceed his grasp?"

Communicating To Save Time

Poor communication is one the biggest time wasters, and yet communication is an area that is often neglected. Most communication experts agree that few of us communicate clearly. Clear communication is probably the biggest global and organizational hurdle businesses face. Often individuals ignore the warning signs of the poor transfer of messages because they certain that they are communication adequately.

Most people believe that they have the process down pat, since they've been communicating, since, roughly, age one. After all, it's only common sense. Communication, though, clearly takes desire and skill.

Four Challenges to Better Communication

There are four critical challenges to communicating effectively, according to communication experts. The first is called, tongue-twistedly, The Principle of Transactional Verticality. Picture a meeting where a colleague asks, "Do you think I got my point across?" You thought they delivered their message with all the aplomb of an invading swat team, and only howitzers would have made it more forceful. Transactional verticality has occurred; research indicates that in communicating, people have a natural tendency to either charge into the other person with an intimidating style, or act meek and gentle, inviting the other person to charge into them. Standing up straight while communicating is difficult, but necessary. It's only when both parties are standing in balance that clear communication occurs, and the communication exchange respects the opinions of both parties.

The Second Challenge: Silent Agreement

The second challenge to communication is falling into the trap of silent agreement. How often do you bob your head to show attention to a speaker, valiantly assuring them you're not asleep? Those "active listening" skills often convey to the speaker that you're agreeing with their comments and opinions. Later, if you disagree, the speaker may become surly, and offended by your "turncoat" behavior. After all, they reason, they were reading your affirmative, agreeing, non-verbal body language!

The Third Challenge: Facial Expression and Voice Tone

The third challenge is non-verbal communication. Unless you possess a wonderfully, poker face, your facial expressions give away about 55% of your feelings. Your tone of voice accounts for about 38% of your message and your verbal message only rates a 7% effect in delivering a message. Be conscious of what your face and body are saying, and don't minimize their impact.

The Fourth Challenge: Mind Reading

The fourth challenge to communication might be called the crystal ball theory of communicating. Don't get into "management by mind-reading." If you're unsure of a message, it's best to go directly to the source and ask, in a non-threatening way, about your interpretation. Ask a question or two for clarification. Your communicator can lie through their clenched teeth: "Of course, I'm not angry with you," they scowl. Alternatively, they can clear up the muddy message, and save you from perfecting your mind-reading skills.

Good communication takes practice, and pays off in saving you time and misunderstandings.

Time for Boss's Day

The third week of October always celebrates National Boss Day. Suspicious employees may grouse that the day is a devious attempt by bosses to get cards, candy and other signs of homage. The day was actually created in 1958 by an employee to honor her benevolent boss. Since then, card sales have averaged over 1 million cards annually. Boss's Day is a strange phenomenon; it reminds us that the boss-employee relationship has always been an important one. It's critical to make the relationship into a two-way partnership, that benefits both you and your boss.

Getting Praise From Your Boss

One of the major complaints about bosses is the lack of praise and support. If your boss is from the "your paycheck is your reward" school of management, don't despair. You simply have to work harder to let your boss know that praise and feedback motivate you to do your job better. First, make certain that your work really is of high enough quality to deserve the praise and recognition you want. Showing up to work and looking vaguely interested usually doesn't qualify for gratitude from the boss.

Marketing Your Work

Second, find ways to let your boss know about your triumphs and successes. This strategy often makes most employees skittish, and they often discount this type of job behavior, by labeling it "apple-polishing." For your career success its critical to develop a comfort level with publicizing your job accomplishments. After all, your boss and col-leagues know all about your mistakes, it makes sense that they should see the positive side of your work as well.

Time For Boss's Day

1. To get praise from a boss, make certain your work is of high enough quality to merit praise—then re-enforce your boss when you hear positive comments.
2. Find ways to bring attention to your work. (Its career mar-keting—not apple-polishing!)
3. Publicize your work accom-plishments on a larger scale in your organization. Let other departments and units know about your work and its benefits.

Using Praise As Leverage

When you do receive praise from a boss, no matter how minuscule, use the opportunity to tell your boss that praise and recognition keeps you on track as to what she or he expects. Falling to your knees and kissing the hem of their business suits is not recommended in the current business culture.

More Self Marketing Ideas

Publicize your successes and triumphs on a larger scale in your organization. Ask your boss if upper management would be interested in your latest accomplishment; utilize the company newsletter, e-mail, and bulletin boards. Some industrious individuals create internal reports detailing exact-ly how their department's activities benefit other depart-ments; they float copies to their colleagues and their bosses, making it into a type of individualized annual report. Make certain that if you undertake any of this type of career publicity, you are relatively caught up with your ongoing work projects. It's difficult to explain to a boss that you were so busy on your personal public relations campaign that you just didn't have time to do your work. Bosses can be strange in that way.

Favor Time

Do you know that asking a colleague for a favor will strengthen your work relationship? We probably don't give much rational thought to the process.

But why ask a favor? In one fell swoop, you can compliment the other person, and begin building a work partnership. After all, you're asking colleagues for advice, or, for their ability to get something done. You are also setting up an alliance, because now, you owe the other individual, and in repaying the favor, you are building a relationship. Most individuals in the workplace are willing to do favors for others, but often do not take the proactive step of asking others to do favors for them.

The Positive Side of Favors

Many individuals lean toward the inclination of being "too nice" and not saying no to requests that are inconvenient or time-consuming. You may find yourself responding to requests even if your swamped and overwhelmed at work. But the good news is that you can bond and cement relationships by asking favors.

Asking For Favors: Reason Two

Businessman extraordinaire Malcolm Forbes probably put it best when he said: "It's being asked that pleases the most." Asking favors signals that you value another's opinion. Asking a colleague to critique your meeting behavior may be helpful for you to get input about your behavior. Secondly, asking for favors makes the person asked feel important to be included. "I would be more comfortable if Bill could look over the project and tells us if he sees some snags," you might propose. Note that this isn't blatant apple-polishing, but rather a favor, couched in terms that are complimentary. Even if Bill turns you down, the compliment has still been delivered.

Asking For Favors: Reason Three

The third reason to ask for favors is: asking favors not only makes the person asked feel valuable and effective, but also can have a powerful impact on the people who see you ask. Remember, asking opinions or advice makes someone feel valued, and raises their status in front of others, so doing it publicly, can get the effect you desire. (We're referring here to advice and suggestions in this instance, rather than, say a request for half a million dollars.)

Asking others for favors also allows you to use the time management concept of not doing everything yourself, which is a straight and certain path to failure. Asking others for a different approach or idea also helps to stimulate your own thinking, like an incubator for new ideas. Take the time to ask for favors. It's worth it.

Favor Time

1. You can bond and cement work relationships by asking favors.

2. Colleagues feel complimented when you ask for work advice, and value their input.

3. Make certain you repay the favors you ask, and keep a open eye for situations where you can trade favors.

Crisis Time

Time management experts tell us that it takes three times the effort to correct a mistake than to do it right the first time. Unfortunately, a great many individuals operate in this mode of "time management-by-crisis". They spend the majority of their time putting out fires, dousing mistakes, and mopping-up.

The negative side to excessive fire-fighting is that it makes mincemeat out of your schedule. It effectively displaces priorities and keeps you in state of stress arousal; it can eventually burnout even the most dedicated workers. How do you control for crises in the workplace?

Creating Excitement

First, make certain, crises and fire-fighting are not a way to create excitement. Perversely enough, a "hurry-up" mentality loves the rush of impending disasters; a crisis mobilizes and energizes them. Some bosses fit this profile, and use crises, real or manufactured to create teamwork among the troops.

Anticipation and Planning

Second, good management skills allow you to anticipate serious problems and prevent them from happening. It doesn't mean you have to operate from a gloom and doom mind set, but it does mean that there should be some serious planning in place. Crises can then be significantly controlled and eliminated.

The Boss As Crisis-Creator

What if crisis management is effectively orchestrated by your boss, and you find yourself constantly in the maelstrom of the problem? If more than 15% of your time is spent fire-fighting, then there are some obvious problems. Planning and organizing skills need to be mobilized. Start keeping a baseline of

Crisis Time

1. Make certain the crisis you are responding to is not generated by boredom, and the need to play hurry up.
2. Anticipation and planning skills (of a worse case scenario) helps you to avert crisis and emergencies.
3. Head your boss off at the pass with concrete steps to cope with the latest crisis.
4. Hone your crisis-handling skills: you'll use them often.

the crises: when do they occur, and what caused the problem? At some point, you can share the results with your boss in an objective, non-emotional manner. Keep in mind that it is harder to refute evidence that is methodically recorded, dated and analyzed. Even if you know that many of this crises have your boss's helping hand, you can still offer to help solve them in a professional manner. Use "we"-statements, and talk about crises as a shared problem, not just the boss's problem. Point out that you know your boss is concerned about crises that eat up valuable time. (Under no circumstances, do you snicker or chortle at your own brazen utterances. You are not engaged in duplicity, but rather, strategic diplomacy.)

Don't let resentment of the crisis-maker keep you from

being a crisis solver. Philosopher Friedrich Nietzche observed that "Nothing on earth consumes a man more quickly than the passion of resentment."

On to those crises that are calling you!

Managing Your Boss

You're convinced that your boss uses MBBA, Management BY Bumbling Around. Co-workers regale one another daily with choice bits of office hearsay—all true, of course, about your boss's strange habits and peccadilloes. The entire workplace oozes with team spirit; however, its all generated by one common, rallying cry: your boss is terminally weird. Sound like your workplace? Whether you're blessed with a decent boss, or one who needs a serious remedial overhaul, its in your best interest to learn to manage your boss.

Developing Boss Handling Skills

Managing your boss is both the sub-ordinates's duty and in the sub-ordinate's self interest to make the boss as effective and achieving as possible, claims management expert Peter F. Drucker in *Managing For the Future* (Dutton) Drucker encourages you to ask your boss What do I do, and what do my people do that helps you do your job? The second question to ask is: "What do we do that hampers you and makes life more difficult for you?"

Walter Keichel, author of *Office Hours* (Perennial) likens this questioning as a form of intellectual medicine ball with your boss. As you bounce questions off your boss, you're negotiating a work contract with your boss.

Asking For Work Critiques

You may be gun shy about asking your boss for critiques of your performance. It may be that your boss is already an accomplished sniper, and you don't want to give her or him a clearer target. The advantage of asking a boss for feedback on

> ## Questions to Ask Your Boss: (according to Peter F. Drucker)
>
> 1. What do I do, and what do my people do that helps you do your job?
> 2. What do we do that hampers you and makes life more difficult for you?

what hinders them from performing well is that you are controlling the conversation, and you can prepare yourself to hear some criticism about your own performance. Your boss gets the message that you're interested and concerned about both your performance. Although you may never feel comfortable asking this boss to formally mentor you, you can still operate as a team.

Your Boss Is The Roadblock To Promotion

If you have difficulty establishing rapport with your boss, for what ever reason, keep mindful of the fact that you also need the entire organization for your career growth. While it is advantageous to have your boss in your corner, your boss should not be your sole and total source of motivation and career advancement potential. Individuals who have had the misfortune to have unsupportive or unconcerned bosses have often learned new career skills: how to regain control of their career mobility by using their own marketing skills to promote their upward mobility.

As Peter Druker reminds us, your job is not to reform the boss, not to re-educate the boss, not to make the boss conform to what the business schools and management books say bosses should be like. It is to enable a particular boss to be able to perform as a unique individual.

Fire Fighting Time

Every major forest fire across the country produces dozens of media interviews with fire-fighters, coping with the horrendous blazes. Viewers marvel at firefighters expertise in strategizing how to extinguish massive fires. In a similar fashion, an everyday work week consists of "fire-fighting" — putting out problems that flare up.

If you spend your time fire-fighting, and yet have no union card, you have probably vowed to cut down on fire-fighting behaviors. Next emergency, you won't come running with the fire buckets; you will plan a more orderly problem solution.

Four Elements in Firefighting

First: A Real Crisis

Four insights that might change your perceptions about fire-fighting. The first insight is that crisis are usually created by stress junkies: those workers who love the rush and adrenaline of pressure. The crisis may be real, and of real importance to the workplace, but chances are, it's been created by procrastination or simply lack of urgency toward deadlines on the part of the crisis makers. Firefighting thrives on a sense of panic, and adrenaline rushes. Keep calm so you can objectively gauge how real the crisis actually is.

Second: Don't Get Caught Up in The Frenzy

Secondly, you do not have to share the emotions of the crisis maker. Even if you decide to help fight the fire, you can still maintain your own perspective, and decide how much time you are willing to take away from your own priorities.

Third: Keep Your Own Pace

The third factor is that you need to keep your own equilibrium. Crisis makers are invariably procrastinators who need the deadline to serve as an executioner. Get in front of the crisis maker; do your portion ahead of time, and when they fly in with last minute crises, you have some breathing room. (Sure, it isn't fair, but at least you're not sucked into an adrenaline rush you don't want!)

Fire fighting is an expensive way to get things done, in both real costs and emotional ones. Overtime and special services rack up additional bills, while the routine business of the workplace gets ignored. The aftermath of a crisis usually leaves behind battered and exhausted workers.

Fourth Strategy: Don't Reward the Guilty

The fourth strategy is to work with your bosses and co-workers so "fire fighting" or crisis management is not rewarded.

Fire Fighting Time

1. Fire-fighting thrives on a sense of panic and anxiety—whether the crisis is real or trumped-up.
2. Tell yourself that you don't have to get automatically caught up in the frenzy of the crisis.
3. It may be hard, but keep your own equilibrium. Out-guess the crisis-maker and do work ahead.
4. Make certain your workplace and boss do not reward the fire-fighting behavior; try to encourage crisis prevention, instead.

Oftentimes, the crisis creator gets kudos for pulling off a tough assignment. If you join in the praise, you are guaranteed that the behavior will be repeated. Remember Psychology 101? Praise and reward re-in force behavior. Point out that the crisis did not have to have occurred in the first place, and you furthermore, you will be more amenable to helping next time, in a more timely fashion. Save your firefighting skills for real fires.

CHAPTER 7

Quick Organization Strategies

The Clean Desk Imperative

A clean desk is the sign of a clean desk. You wont find than emblazoned on a plaque in a gift shop, because it defies current thinking. A clean desk is most often viewed as a benchmark of efficiency. At one legendary Fortune 500 company, desks had to be cleared at 5:00 PM, or you had an automatic tete-a-tete with your supervisor. Other companies claim that desktops need to be empty so the cleaning crews can polyurethane them, or such, every night. (Have you honestly heard of a cleaning crew clamoring to have more to clean? More likely, its the doings of upper management, rather than some obsessive-compulsive janitorial staff.)

> **The Clean Desk Imperative:**
>
> 1. Clean desks do not mean you're efficient. You may simply be adept as shoveling everything out of sight.
> 2. Find a desk style that fits for you. If you need to leave work out in plain view, then develop a system of better reminders, than work piles.
> 3. Furnish your work space with some office supply bins, trays, and in-baskets.
> 4. Re-arrange and design a work space that helps maintain your productivity and keeps your work moving.

Does Your Desk Measure Up?

What exactly does a clean desk signify? Business magazines love to create gorgeous layouts, showcasing the offices of successful executives. The desks are always splendid affairs, ranging from priceless antiques to sleek, Plexiglas models. The copy usually reads: Olivia loves to work at her seventeenth century French desk, where its said Emperor Napoleon penned love notes to his Josephine. The desk is virtually empty, except for some well-chosen bibelots. The message is clear: successful folk have clean desks. Undoubtably, they also have secretaries who fetch such distasteful items as files, reports, and pink message slips. These magazine layouts have one purpose: to make you feel inadequate and possibly suicidal about your own desk.

Desk Styles and Efficiency

To lower your stress level about your desk, keep these truths in mind: A clean desk is not a moral imperative. Well-organized people can have messy desks. Inefficient folk can have desks that are scrupulously clean. Neither desk style guarantees work efficiency.

Many times, the over-loaded desk functions as a memory-nudger. Folders, phone messages, samples, and other paraphernalia on the desk function as a physical reminder to do something. If it's in plain sight, there's a higher probability of action. Conversely, if items are tucked way in drawers, its akin to sealing them in a time capsule; they may be unearthed in the next decade or so.

Take a sojourn to an office supply store. Load up on plastic bins, dividers, stationery caddies and compartmentalized trays for notes. Any type of workstation organizer will help. Wall space can be utilized with hanging bins or envelopes to route work. Organizational experts are divided about the use of bulletin boards: they either love them or hate them. If not policed regularly, bulletin boards can begin to resemble billboards in a decaying neighborhood, with layers and layers of peeling paper. One alternative is instead, to place must-see items in clear zippered bags, the kind used for children's pencils.

The solution to the clean desk controversy is to design a workplace that is functional for your individual needs. Your own desk may never be profiled in a glossy magazine, but it shouldn't stop you from creating a desk that is user friendly.

RX For Your Desk

Own up to it: your desk looks like a toxic waste dump. Admittedly, the picketers haven't shown up yet, but there is no clean space on your desk. It's estimated that 60% of the papers piled up on a desk have little value or meaning.

Two Reasons for Desk Clutter

Most of it collects because of two reasons: first, is "out of sight, out of mind." If you stuff something in a drawer you will forget it completely; planted on your desk, you have a constant reminder. (If you can see it, that is!)

The second reason for desk clutter is lack of decision-making. Instead of deciding what to do with incoming memos, mail, or reports, it gets added it to the pile — and quickly forgotten.

If your desk is cluttered, you're not working as efficiently and productively as you could be. Eliminate the clutter, and you'll save thirty minutes a day, simply because you'll be able to find all the unfinished work that has been lying around in piles, untouched, on your desk.

You are probably going to need two hours of uninterrupted time to deal with a dis-

> **RX for Your Desk**
>
> 1. Eliminate desk top clutter and you'll save thirty minutes per day.
> 2. Take two hours per day to dig out a disastrous work area.
> 3. Designate a (1) keeper pile and a (2) throw pile.
> 4. Create a Master List for all your projects, and add to it daily, making certain that no items fall between the cracks.

aster area desk. Make an appointment with yourself, close the door, and have your phone monitored. Divide papers into a keeper pile and a throw away pile. For the items in the keeper file, ask yourself what action needs to be taken? Is the paper to be re-routed to someone else, does a phone call need to be made, or does the paper need a file folder?

Creating a Master List

Lest some items be relegated to the Black Hole of File Drawers, the item needs to be listed on your Master List. On looseleaf paper, make a Master List, which will become an inventory of all your unfinished work and ongoing projects, and future tasks you'd like to accomplish. Note that this is not a daily to do list; "Pick up dog at the vet's" does not belong on this Master List because this its a task that will be accomplished quickly, and get crossed off your daily to do list. The Master List should be placed somewhere easily accessible, like a top drawer. Write on every line of the list, and do not enumerate. Priorities are not important at this point; what is most crucial, is that every project gets listed.

Since the idea is not to dream up new time-consuming tasks, don't rewrite your Master List every day. When a project is finished, cross off that item. You'll be able to monitor your progress as well as you look back on completed tasks.

When you've completed about 50% of the items on the first page of your list, transfer the remaining items to a new page. The idea is to cull your lists, and make certain no items get sandwiched in and forgotten. Date your old lists, and if you're really compulsive, make a file labeled "Old Lists." Make certain they carry a delete date however, so you're not just stockpiling clutter.

Be warned that a clean desk may erroneously signal to your co-workers that you've been fired, and just cleared off your desk. Bear with the taunts and slings: it will pay off with higher productivity. Add that to your Master List!

Paper Shuffling 101

Do you dream of replacing your in box with a trash dumpster--the mini-ton variety? One of the few certainties of our worklife is the constantly replenished in-box. It's very much like hangers in your closet: you would have sworn you cleaned them out, and now they've returned in huge masses. Likewise, in-boxes just keep filling up. To keep yours under control a few rules are in order. An in-box cannot function as a Lost and Found for orphan papers; that's how in-boxes become sky-high. You need a paper shuffling system that substitutes for simply dumping new paperwork into your in-box.

Sorting Paperwork

The organization experts differ on their approaches, but all agree that paperwork eventually has to be sorted. You need to designate a holding area for paperwork that needs to be sorted. You can use "Sort" trays, baskets or just designated spots on a table or desk. (Those of you who believe in the Law of Vertical Surfaces, where every available spot will eventually be occupied by some clutter, will shudder at this offer of sorting refuges.) However, a warning is in order; you need a "daily sort": a commitment to sort often, and you cannot use the sort piles as just another place to pile renegade papers. Use the same sort spots consistently.

Four Rules for Paperwork

Stephanie Winston, author of *The Organized Executive* (Warner Books, 1985) advises using the TRAF system, arguing that there are only 4 and $^1/_2$ things you can do with paper: Toss, refer, act, file and the item, is read it. Winston maintains that the trick of paper mastery is to make each piece of paper yield an action. Read gets only a $^1/_2$ designation since any paper that takes longer than a few minutes to read belongs in a separate folder or a tray labeled Business or Personal Reading. You can designate a portable reading file that you carry to kill time waiting for appointments, and in drive-through lines.

Remember that briefcases are not mobile storage facilities. Although your paperwork may enjoy a ride in your car, chances are, dumping unsorted paperwork into a briefcase, simply makes you feel active and virtuous. It does not get further along in your paper system.

> **Paper Shuffling 101**
>
> 1. Designate a holding area for paperwork in transit.
>   Use sort tray's, baskets, or in-boxes.
> 2. Use Winston's TRAF system
>   Toss
>   Refer
>   Act
>   File
>   (Read)
> 3. Use a Hot File for current projects, tickets, and meeting notices, and reminders.
>   Use a Cold File for future or pending projects.
> 4. Put delete dates on all files.

Hot and Cold Files

The simplest, and most bulky system of paper sorting consists of using a "hot" and "cold" files. "Hot" files contain everything that you need for this week's activities.

"Cold" files may be future projects, or items that carry discard dates. Eventually cold projects either heat up, or get banished to further cold storage, the larger filing systems or archives.

Whatever system you use, make certain your in-box does not become the graveyard where old papers go to die.

Four Rules for Organizing Your Possessions

You don't want to appear paranoid, but it's the third time this week your car keys are missing. Now you can't find your checkbook. Two days ago your utility bill had given you the slip. Feeling like a detective in a third-rate mystery, you wonder if you're seeing a pattern emerge. You are, and it's called disorganization. Misplacing your possessions, and not being able to find crucial information are frustrating activities that rob you of time and peace of mind.

Bertrand Russell once wrote: "It is the preoccupation with possession more than anything else, that prevents men from living freely and nobly." Obviously, Bertrand had the same problems with his keys. How do you get around these nagging, but everyday problems? The answer lies in applying some organizational tactics to deal with your possessions. Organization sometimes looms in our minds as an eight-hour, uninterrupted project that if we had the time to do, we wouldn't be disorganized in the first place. Oftentimes, it's much more simple.

Organization Strategies: The First Rule

Organization can be improved with a few simple strategies: first, have a place for everything, and everything in its place. Your grandmother probably drove you crazy with this homily, but its solid time management. When you misplace something, it's often a commonly used item that you don't think about consciously, like keys. They may be in the door, on top of the mail, or in the refrigerator, because you put away the milk on your way in. Using the place for everything theory, you would train yourself to automatically place keys in one spot, so it would eventually become an unconscious habit.

The Second Rule

The second rule of organization is to return items to their place. For example, it's counterproductive to gather all your office-type supplies in one spot, and then carry off the stapler to the basement, never to be seen again. Master the rule of returning items to their home.

The Third Rule

The third rule of organization is to get rid of clutter. Clutter experts suggest that clutter serves to depress us, keeps us from organizing our possessions, and helps us, furthermore, to lose things because of the clutter. If you're part of the genus pack-rat, you know how hard it is to wrench yourself from your possessions, and the belief that your might need something — sometime. You might try moving your clutter into the twentieth century by photographing it, putting

---

Four Rules for Organizing Your Possessions

1. A place for everything and everything in its place.
2. Master the rule: return items to their place when you're through with them.
3. Get rid of clutter: it slows you down and makes organization time costly.
4. Log your possessions and their locations in a notebook. Clear up your mind for more important details.

---

its location on computer, or videotaping it. Then you can dispose of it, knowing it can stay with you for eternity, or at least until your disc wears out.

The Fourth Rule

The fourth simple way to organize yourself is to keep a small notebook as a directory to your possessions. If you realize you'll never remember the whereabouts of concert tickets in two months, write their location in your notebook. Nail, staple, or adhere the notebook to the inside of a cabinet door. It may seem idiotic to you, but why clutter up your brain with trivia that can be retrieved? If you try to keep track of magazine articles, make yourself a reading log with the pertinent dates and issues.

Disorganization can be conquered in your lifetime!

Re-Thinking Your Work Space

There are those who greet the change of seasons with ebullient spirits, and see it as a good time to put their life in order. Others would hibernate through the rest of the winter if they could, peeping out when the winter doldrums are over. Since we can't mimic the bears, we can look at some strategies that could help us organize our disorder. Start slowly. As you look at your desk, work space, or living quarters, ask yourself: "What might make things better now?" You're not asking for perfection, or the final solution for disorganization, but rather a starting point for your organizing efforts. If money was no object, what would your work space include? This creative day-dreaming helps you to sort out your priorities.

Rethinking Your Work Space

1. Survey your work domain. What would make things easier for you?
2. Try picking up your work area ten minutes per day.
3. Find a system that works. A place to process papers; permanent places for revolving items; containers to house odds and ends, make more efficient use of storage space. Buy duplicates of things you use often.
4. Most importantly: keep it simple, so you'll use it!

Getting Started

Next, ease into the job. Although you may be discouraged that you have tons of paraphernalia to put in place, try picking up just ten minutes a day. (Otherwise, you'll feel overwhelmed.) At work, take a fast ten minutes before you scoot out for an appointment. At home, you may try picking up a room during commercials, while glued to the TV set.

Finding A System

Don't get too complex. Adopt systems that are easy, convenient and simple. Otherwise, you wont use your own system. Consider larger wastebaskets: organizational experts note that individuals throw away more when they have larger waste containers, so obviously, they encourage pitching. Use hampers where you peel off your clothes. Think in multiples: you may become more organized with more places to stash things. Visit one of the many container/organization stores that are springing up like mushrooms. Window shopping can give scores of ideas for stashing and corralling possessions.

Keeping Motivated

Motivate yourself with rewards and incentives because there is a tendency to get discouraged easily as you look at your surroundings, and realize you haven't reached the nirvana of neatness and organization. Reward yourself as you make some progress. You may also motivate yourself by setting a target deadline to work toward, such as inviting people over, or designate a specific holiday when things will be completed.

Time for Clutter

Do humans have a inherited DNA gene impels them to fill up every available space with paper? Many paper and clutter experts maintain that the top culprit in cluttering up our lives is paper. (You just thought it was your moth-eaten moose head from college!) Ask yourself the telling question: how many pieces of paper do you deal with a day? Your answer will probably be grossly underestimated, as we overlook papers like magazines, receipts, tickets, shopping lists, coupons, checks, and photos, in addition to junk mail, and work files. The typical person paws through 100 to 250 pieces of paper per day! Multiply that by 365 days per year, and you can see how you can become inundated with paper very quickly.

> ### Time for Clutter
>
> 1. Stop collecting paper at its source.
> 2. Don't categorize paper into too many categories at your initial sorting process. Try for larger categories until you have made a first pass through all you paperwork.
> 3. Be ruthless; throw as you go.
> 4. File papers only if you have a clear reason for keeping them. Ask yourself "Can I live without this?"

Rule #1: Reducing Paper Volume

The most expedient and fastest remedy for paper trails is to stop collecting paper at its source. The biggest bottleneck in the paper backup is the tendency to pile papers sort or organize later. With paper, putting it into stacks is an invitation to simply store paper. You're doomed if you start categorizing into too many options (like sort later, put in archives, scrapbook, consider further, wait to see if it's important.) To get on top of your paper become ruthless: crumble up your paperwork into a large wastebasket. No fair creeping back hours later with remorse, and dragging the remnants back into your life!

Rule #2 for Paper

The second rule is to not let a paper into the system (filing cabinet, To-Do file, in-box) unless you are clear about its purpose. You may be wasting your time filing information you will never need, and cluttering up your valuable file space.

Rule #3 for Sorting

Another way to control paper clutter is to spread it all out at once and dig in. Don't nibble: empty out entire boxes and drawers. A caution is in order however, just because something can be sorted into a category, doesn't mean it's worth keeping. The final questions to ask at this de-cluttering impasse: is "Can I live without this paperwork? How much trouble is it to replace it, if necessary?"

The Paper Glut

The average American will handle more than 460 pounds of paper a year. That's almost 20% more than the volume of ten years ago. Yet, it wasn't long ago that futurists were predicting the "paperless office" of tomorrow. Why doesn't that "paperlessness" translate to your desk or home?

One of the reasons we seem to be overwhelmed with paper has to do with the exponential growth of paper and the complex nature of decisions people make from day to day. Organizing consultants have pointed out that the growth of catalog, direct mail campaigns, and faxes have added to our paper piles.

Your Daily Mail Dilemma

Incoming mail is another culprit in the paper wars. If you've recently subscribed to new magazines or journals, you know your mailbox will never suffer the pangs of emptiness again. Direct mail offers have become so polished and slick, that a rapid perusal of your mail no longer suffices; you probably find yourself opening more complex mail than in the past. Experts differ on whether to stockpile junk mail, and then leisurely pore over it while watching TV, or chatting on the phone, or take the more direct route of dispatching mail quickly, everyday. The advantage of stockpiled mail, is that a few days time makes much of it less important, and it may be thrown out decisively. If you don't isolate a specific place for daily bills and solicitations, and then couple it with indecisiveness, you will invariably add to your clutter level daily.

Daily Desk Wars Against Paper

Another factor in paper build-up is that the average professional's desk is estimated to hold about 36 hours work of work on it at any given time, unless of course, the afore mentioned professional is a born-again clean desk convert. Despite what the slogan signs say, a messy desk is the sign of reduced work efficiency. Piles of unfinished work tend to overwhelm, rather than act as reminders; the sheer volume of clutter makes losing an important paper or file all the more likely.

Four Strategies for Reducing Clutter

Clutter experts believe that disorganized people need to set goals, make plans, keep a record, and most importantly, keep things simple. If you categorize yourself on the extreme end of the disorganizational scale, then you have to be careful of your inclinations; don't add organizing paraphernalia that you wont use because it is too complex. If you're suspicious of a complicated day-planner, for example, trust your intuition. No matter how dazzling it may be, if you don't see yourself using it, its just another distraction. Opt for a spiral notebook.

The Paper Glut

1. Make decisions about paper everyday.
2. Daily mail needs to be policed.
3. Set goals for organizing your clutter.

Makes plans.

Keep a record of files, possessions, important paperwork.

Keep your system simple.

Time Wasters

What are the time robbers in your day? Most individuals will name long staff meetings, the telephone, and waiting for others to deliver on promises. Notice how this list points the finger of blame towards other people? Most time management studies back up this assertion: most individuals do not blame their own habits for the time that eludes them. Usually, the blame is placed on uncontrollable events, such as boring staff meetings, or difficult co-workers or fellow departments.

Major Time Wasters

1. Taking extended breaks and lunches.
2. Saying yes too many times to co-workers; your own work gets left undone.
3. Phone calls that take longer than necessary to conduct business. (Watch for boredom on your part!)
4. No systematic follow-through on projects. Details slip through the cracks because there is no way to track odds and ends.

The reality is, most time wasters are made up of small spurts of time, and are usually connected to our own behaviors. This is the crux of time management: to control your time, you need to take control over the time that is within your control. Since we have minimal control over other people, it makes sense to target our typical, daily time wasters. These are the activities we can change or modify.

Time Waster #1: Work Slow-Downs

The first time waster is over-extended breaks and lunches. Part of the rationalization, is that we deserve some minimal pleasure during the day, and chit-chatting with co-workers "humanizes" the workplace. This may be true, but you may be squandering your high concentration and high energy time on a donut and caffeine infusion. You may also be slowing down your morning pace, or interrupting your work flow, by the wrong break at the wrong time.

Time Waster # 2: Saying Yes

Another time waster is the inability to say no. Maybe you fall prey to a nice co-worker, who always needs your help in a crunch, only the crunches seem to come more and more, frequently. Start laying some boundaries by announcing early in the week that you have many high-priority tasks that need precedence the next few days. Follow-up by saying no, firmly. If you tend to over-commit yourself, write some index cards with warning messages; tape these to your desk and phone.

Time Waster # 3: Phone Time

Get a mirror and an egg-timer for your phone. The mirror is to watch your facial gestures as you practice charming, diplomatic ways to end phone conversations gracefully. The egg-timer is used to see how quickly you can wrap up routine calls, and cut back on your overall phone conversations. The egg timer will remind you to minimize the social side of the calls, and the mirror will reflect growing impatience, if you begin to lose control of the call. It may not seem like much, but you can probably shave five minutes, from every call.

Estimate ten calls a day, and you will have gained almost an hour in previously "lost" time.

Time Waster #4: Follow Through

Another time waster is having no follow up system on your projects. You can devise a system as casual as affixing a certain color of sticky-note to the outside of a folder that indicates some follow-up is in order: a phone call, a summary wrap-up due in two weeks, or invoice to mail, for example. Date your sticky note, and move the folders to your "hot" (take action) file section. If you use a daily or weekly tickler system, place the reminder in your ticker file. Note on your daily calendar some warning signals on follow-tasks, so you aren't lambasted some foggy, Monday morning with an inflexible deadline.

You'll probably find more time wasters in your daily life that you can attack and control, but the critical step to finding time robbers is to control behaviors in your own domain.

Finding Filed Information

November marks the anniversary of the opening of King Tutankhamen's tomb in Luxor, Egypt in 1922. The entire world was electrified by the reports of rich artifacts and beautiful treasures that had been preserved since 1352 B.C. King "Tut" became an overnight sensation. Long-forgotten Egyptian tombs bear a striking similarity to some of our own file drawers: usually nothing has been unearthed in years. Secondly, the "artifacts" sealed within, have some mysterious and significant function — but no one is certain what it is. Third, it usually takes a major expedition to uncover the files, and requires an enormous outlay of time. There is also the possibility that you may never uncover what you think should be there.

Deciphering Your Files

Experts differ on their file advice. We're probably most concerned with files that we deal with on a regular basis: our own desk files, at home files, and files we create, hoping to make sense of polyglot materials. Time management expert Stephanie Winston suggests that a good retrieval system should only require three minutes to find a file or paper. Broad and generic headings should also be used. A file labeled "New mailing lists" has the potential for being lost forever in the files, since you'll search under mailing or lists.

A Numerical Filing System

Some organizational experts point out that manila file

Finding Filed Information

1. Create broad and generic names for your files that you'll recognized six months later.
2. Numerical filing systems can be as simple as assigning the number "100" to files on your hobby, "200" to antique car information, and so on.
3. Don't save it if you can't find it later!

folders and supplies are cheap, compared to the time you waste searching for items you have misfiled. But most individuals do not have the finely honed skills of an executive secretary, and become perplexed by filing. One solution for those hard-to-find file items is to use a variation of the library systems: give categories a numerical system. Perhaps your three hobbies are racquetball, antique cars and gardening, and you have odd bits of information that defies categorization. Racquetball files would carry a 100 designation, 102 for racquetball equipment, 103 for an article on form. Antique cars would carry a 200 designation and gardening information, a 300. A folder would be placed in front of each hobby category, carrying the consecutive numbers and contents, serving as a file inventory. Sound like a lot of work? Possibly, but if you deplore of ever locating the clipping on trimming your evergreens, then starting a system will eventually pay off when, voila, you retrieve exactly what you saved. Archeological expeditions need to be kept to burial tombs--not carried out daily in file drawers.

Duplicate Time

The perfect time management fantasy: an army of clones who would attend to the time consuming, but necessary functions of one's life. Boring meetings, busy work and long lines could all be managed by robotic extras, leaving us to exert our energies on higher level of activities like, well, sun-bathing. Where are those inventive scientists when we need them?

Using Duplication

Fantasies aside, the idea of duplication is still a great time management tool. Consider your everyday activities: how many of them could be streamlined by using duplication? In the category of search missions, how much time do you spend looking for everyday items like keys and eyeglasses? Have extra sets made. Cynics will scoff that now you have a new problem: misplacing 17 sets of car keys instead of just a few. Optical companies will thrive making duplicate spectacles. Consider the rule of duplication: does an "extra" of something streamline your life, and reduce frustration? If so, then the "extra" is a necessity. One manager, who travels often in her job, bit the bullet and bought duplicates of all her toiletries and make-up. Knowledgeable folk know that this is roughly equivalent to buying a good used car, but the executive claims it has paid off handsomely in stress and time reduction. Another seasoned traveler swears by canned tunafish and a can-opener in her carry-on bag—sort of like C-rations for the complete business traveler.

Second Rule of Duplication

The second rule of duplication is to restock your stores. You're right back to ground-zero if you don't replenish your extras. A current comedian claims that the rise of huge warehouse groceries not only saves us time, but allows us to buy enough food to invite entire foreign countries over for snacks.

Duplicate grocery lists, drug and hardware store lists, office supply lists, children's chore lists, and any other activity performed on a regular basis.

> ## Duplicate Time
>
> 1. The first rule of duplication: does having extras of something streamline your life and reduce frustration?
> 2. The second rule of duplication: re-stock your stores.
> 3. Create your own duplicated lists, forms, routing slips, and instruction forms.

Adapt message slips, routing slips and instruction slips to your own needs and have a supply cheaply printed. If you don't like the impersonality of computerized personal letters, then substitute round-robin letters with relatives, where everyone adds on their news, and then forwards it to the next unsuspecting loved one.

Duplicate! It may be a long technological wait for the clones you need.

Paying for Time Help

"It's easier to do it myself," you say, "Why pay someone else?" If it's so easy, why haven't you done it? There are a number of orphan tasks: the odd, the boring and tedious, the messy tasks that need to be accomplished someday, but keep getting pushed off your priority list. These tasks are on the list of other entrancing jobs, like tax audits, cleaning gutters, and root canals.

Throwing In The Towel

At what point do you capitulate? When do you call in re-inforcements, and pay, barter or cajole someone else into doing the task? For many time management types, surrender is anathema. In their minds, paying someone else to do something they are capable of doing is a blatant form of laziness, sloth and moral depravity. There may even be a spiritual side, linking sin and punishment to the dreaded task, but time management theologians are still divided on this issue.

Consider your back yard, which could double for a Tarzan movie set, the garage that eats people, the Rolodex gone berserk, the filing system that needs major overhauling, or the personal paperwork and bills that date back to the Spanish American War. Is it time to call in help? Could you recruit child or teenage labor, and boss a crew? The point is, not to eat up your hard-earned money by hiring every task to be done by others, but, rather, to look at what is not being done, and has a higher likelihood of getting done if hired out. You can also assess tasks into a higher and lower level of skill. Could you be finishing a more challenging task, if someone else was handling the ho-hum tasks?

Getting Volunteers

Do you have organized friends who would love to help you clean out a basement or file system? (The key to discovering such treasured individuals is not to check their linen closets for neatness, but rather, mention your dreaded problem. Neat types usually offer to help organize; they see you as a challenge, a convert, or simply a good way to indulge their fetish.) You can always repay the favor by having them to dinner, giving them a choice, gourmet treat, or by offering to trade your particular skills in return.

In time management, people often have to be at a crisis point before they will delegate tasks. Like cleaning before the cleaning crew arrives, we don't want others to know about our true messiness. A cardinal rule of time management says that we don't have to be doing everything ourselves to be seen as capable. We can let go of tasks that need to be done.

Consider dumping the task. That's right – don't do it at

> ## Paying For Time Help
>
> 1. There is no hard and fast rule as to when to pay for time help. If a task lingers on and on, and your enthusiasm for it lessens with every week, consider hiring it out.
> 2. Can you get your more organized friends to help you organize your files or devise storage space. Throw yourself on their mercy!
> 3. You don't have do be doing every task to be capable.

all. If you've gone this long without doing it, maybe it's one of those endless tasks that simply wont get done. Stifle the guilt and move forward!

Datebook Dementia

In the 1990 movie "Taking Care of Business," one of the main characters loses his Filofax, and ultimately his identity, his status, his marriage, and his job. Filofaxes are the Mercedes Benz of the datebook world. They can contain your life—all those numbers you need, your secret Swiss bank account numbers, the area code for Nepal, your projects, and your sacrosanct appointments. Record your expenses, trigger the memory pages, outline your conversations, and record your exercise progress. A Filofax begins selling for around $180.00 for the stripped down models; extras just require bringing a blank check to your trendy stationers. Glossy magazines often run in-depth interviews with the famous and frantic, who reveal their "highly personal relationship" with their Filo, as the initiates affectionately call them.

> **Datebook Madness**
>
> 1. Use a datebook organizer only if you're committed to using one; otherwise, opt for a simple calendar.
> 2. Datebooks, with their goal setting sections, memory sections, address files, can function as a portable office and keep everything in one spot.
> 3. Have a backup system in case you lose your datebook organizer.

Do you have a Significant Other datebook? Or does the talk of structured calendars make you squirm? Highly scientific research was conducted, first, by hanging out at a office supply store, and secondly, watching the aforementioned film with the Filofax as the main lead. The results? Desperate tales of datebooks gone amok, and disorganized lives.

Two Types of Datebook Users

Datebook usage can be divided into two camps, the Passionates and the Purists. The Passionates are those who have found meaning and purpose to their existence through datebooks. They can be identified by the zealous look and rapturous tone when speaking of their brand name "organizer". You're convinced they're on retainer from the company; at any moment they'll will whip out an order form, and worse, you'll sign it. Passionates find that they can't function without their books. They recognize a significant time management maxim: you don't have to remember everything, as long as you can retrieve it. People who enjoy using organizers like the structure of having to set goals, make lists, and transpose memory reminders with aids like numerical systems. Some even utilize elaborate codes and symbols to note delegation, projects completed, and unfinished.

As the movie "Taking Care of Business" pointed out, there is peril in counting on your book to keep you organized. One executive left her datebook at her hairdressers; she became so crunched for time that for a three-day period she made frantic calls to her hairdresser to ask where she needed to be. The datebook and executive were eventually re-united but the hairdresser, suffering from post traumatic datebook stress, asked the executive to find a new salon.

Datebook Purists

The Purists are those who disdain any type of organized date booking. They may use a small notebook, but it's usually costs about a dollar. Their calendars are the free ones from their credit unions, and they often carry dates in their head rather than writing them down. These are the souls who remember a three month dental checkup for December twenty-sixth. They view the hoopla associated with datebooks as, well, excessive. At best, purists may deign to carry a few blank index cards, but it has to be a fairly special project. They would identify with a survey conducted by a Fortune 500 company who gifted all their management personnel with expensive organizers. One year later, it was revealed that only 20% of the employees used them for anything more than a desk calendar and paperweight. The datebooks faithfully attended all company meetings, however.

Datebook Manners

Whatever your relationship, or lack of one, with a datebook; remember business etiquette. Never write in someone else's book; it's considered far too intimate. Don't brag excessively about your datebook; every other owner thinks their own is special, too. Showing photos of them appears less than business like. Lastly, if you feel your addiction is beyond help, there's probably a clinic somewhere in California that can discreetly help. Mark down the date, and go.

Demoralizing Datebooks

"I really need to get one of those datebook organizers to keep my life in order." This is often the lament of industrious workers who are trying valiantly to corral 137 tiny pieces of paper into order. The paper scraps and envelope backs often constitute their current priorities. The datebook companies have succeeded in making organizers an standard office accessory, but the fact remains: they simply don't work for everyone.

Is A Datebook For You?

Before investing your pension in an organizer, assess whether you're a candidate for one. (To the uninitiated, datebook organizer owners may appear snobbish, clannish and superior. But, remember, this is America: you can buy one if you want!) The first question to ask yourself is, will I actually use one? This may seem very elementary, but individuals often buy them, and engage in a torturous relationship with them. Be honest. Datebooks work only if you write in them consistently, and open them regularly.

Second: What Functions Do You Need?

Secondly, what specialized functions do you need to keep organized? If your day is fragmented, interrupted, and characterized by many shifts in tasks, then you probably need some type of Project Lists. Project Lists sections are offered by many datebook companies, and allow you to record and remember decisions, questions, and follow-up details. You probably need Meeting Notes, to record meeting items, and committee assignments. If someone promises an action in a meeting, you can record what they vowed to do, if your memory fails you, a month later.

Demoralizing Datebooks

1. Determine if you are willing to use a datebook organizer. (You can use a spiral notebook if that's what works for you!)
2. If you do invest in one, shop for one a style that allows you to personalize it to your work and home requirements. Beware of the ones that have you re-copying lists and goals often.
3. Are you a list-maker? If yes, you will love a datebook organizer. If you abhor lists, you'll probably hate the organizer as well.
4. Pick an organizer that has good reminder joggers for details and follow-through.
5. Use it; an organizer is only helpful if you use it daily; they make expensive paperweights if not utilized.

Third: Lists and More Lists

Third, are you a list-maker? Do you work better from massive lists, charting all your tasks? Some individuals actually do better with loose leaf notebooks. They often feel stultified by an organizer and prefer the expansiveness of a do-it-yourself binder. Keep in mind, that many organizers are set up to keep you writing your goals, and priorities, and then re-writing them on other pages. If this seems like a Promethean task to you, then don't bother investing in that style of datebook. You don't need a blank calendar to make you feel guilty everyday!

Fourth: Use Memory Aids

Fourth, consider some type of memory device for your organizer. They vary, but the component that's critical is to have a listing of all the odds and ends of tasks that qualify as grass-catcher tasks. "Take Brutus for flea-dip," and "Comparison shop for insurance prices," may not be raging priorities, but they're still items that you want to remember. Some individuals use the memory lists when they garner an extra hour somewhere. Memory lists may carry 50 - 100 items. They need to be numbered, and dated. Review the memory lists on a regular basis to see if some of those items are heating up—and on their way to becoming high priority items.

Fifth: Datebook Usage

Lastly, an organizer can only be as organized as you are. If you leave your organizer at home, or in the trunk of the car consistently, there's a strong message there. You and your organizer have not bonded properly. Don't worry, there will probably be support groups for these problems. You can stand up and admit: I abuse my datebook. I neglect it, and don't buy it refill pages. Someone else will soothingly say: "It's okay, we've all been there. Now, we just take one calendar day at a time."

INDEX

A

absent-minded, 2

B

bad habits, 5, 6
balance, 41, 51
behavior change, 7
body clock, 103
boredom, 45
bosses, 181, 189
Boss Day, 181
boundaries, 9, 174
burnout, 56, 59-60
breaks, 49
Bright, Deborah, 172
bureaucrats, 131

C

change, 3
clerical work, 36
clutter, 210
communicating, 178
complaining, chronic, 165
concentration, 145
controlling time, 129
creative thinking, 63
creativity, 154
crisis, 60, 186-187, 192

criticism, 172
critiques (of work), 173

D

Dallas Diagnostic
    Association, 31
datebooks, 224, 226
deadly sins (time manage-
    ment), 162
deadlines, 84
decision-making, 129
delegation, 102
details, 107
desks, clean 196, 199
desperation attacks, 42
discipline, 3
disorganization, 207
distractions, 54
discomfort dodging, 78
dog days, 146
drains (time management),
    165
Drucker, Peter, 27, 189
duplicate forms, 220

E

eighty-twenty principle, 122
effective time managers, 94

energy, 46

energy codes, 52-53

estimation, time, 105

English, Gary, 144

extra time, 99

Eyre, Richard & Linda, 41

F

favors, 184

fictitious frontiers (of time), 137

files, 204

filing systems,
  numerical, 217

Filofax, 224

firefighting, 186-193

follow up tactics, 107-108

fragments (of time), 214

G

grass-catcher items, 59, 83

grouping work, 97

goals, 11, 150

H

habits, 7-9

habituation, 143

hassles, 38

high screeners, 54

hot files, 203

humor, 146

I

interruptions, 110, 115
  as time robbers, 113

innovation, 155

J

job performance. 170, 172

juggling, 62

jumpstarting day, 105

K

Keyes, Ralph, 102

Knaus, William J., 77

L

Lavie, Peretz, 64

late behavior, 168

lists, duplicate 219
  master, 199

locus of control, 28

logs (time), 134

lost items, 36

long-range goals, 12

low screeners, 54

M

mail, 212

marketing work, 182

managing bosses, 189

master lists, 199

managers time use, 94

    characteristics, 76

    superior, 58

Mehrabian, Albert, 54

memory, 119

mission statements, 32

motivation, 28, 139

morning routines, 6

multi-tasking, 62

myths (of time), 32

N

negative thinking, 13, 14

negotiation, 174

no, saying, 214

O

organic time, 103

organization,

    four myths, 34

    four rules, 206

    possessions, 89, 205

    work space, 208

    clutter, 210

over-commitment, 129

over-doing, 87

overwork, 56-57

P

panic time, 42

paper,

    glut, 212

    shuffling, 101, 202

    volume, 210

    reduction, 211

paperwork

    grouping, 97

Parkinsons First Law, 22

Pareto Principle, 122

paying for time help, 221

phone time, 215

planning, 152

    60/20 principle, 152, 186

priorities, 26, 44, 60

priority checks, 22-23

posteriorities, 27

possessions

    organizing, 205

procrastination

    battling, 72, 77-79, 81

    escapes, 86-88

    excuses, 74

    ploys, 71

symptoms, 68-69
priorities, 26, 83-84
productivity, 17, 146,
procrastinated tasks, 89
projects, 99

Q
quiet time, 113

R
requests for time, 184
rewards, 8-9, 91
remedial time management, 149
Rossi, Ernest, L., 47

S
sanctuary (from time), 103
saying no, 175
Scott, Dru, 22
self confidence, 28-29
self discipline, 2
self doubt, 77
self marketing, 170
simplifying tasks, 43
sleep, 64
    patterns, 66
    research, 64
    reduction, 65

stimuli (time), 54
stress
    hardiness, 38
    and overwork, 57
success, 50

T
tasks
    juggling, 62-63
    staying power, 107
tickler files, 108
time banking, 158-159
time barriers, 16
time bites, 140
time bits, 97
time detectives, 126
timelock, 102
time logs, 134
time (for yourself), 40
time panic, 42
time pressures, 102
time sickness, 31
time synchronization, 31
time robbers, 114
time wasters, 8. 16, 214
time wish list, 158
to-do lists, 27, 152
tracking time, 19

TRAF system (Stephanie
    Winston), 202
trivial priorities, 24

U
Ultradian rhythms (energy),
    47

V
vanishing time, 19
vital ingredients, 122

W
waiting, 116
Webb & Agnew, 66
Winston, Stephanie, 202
work boredom, 45
    symptoms, 45
    battling, 46
work values, 76
working smarter, 95
work space, 208

X

Y

Z

Training, Seminars, and Keynotes

Could your organization benefit from hearing Dr. Mary Corcoran, The Time Doctor? Dr. Corcoran presents a variety of seminars and keynote speeches based on all phases of time management, productivity, and peak performance. National audiences range from large corporations to small businesses, not for profits, associations, government, muncipal, and state agencies, as well as educational institutions.

To contact Dr. Mary Corcoran, call, write, fax, or e-mail her:

Dr. Mary E. Corcoran
William Waldron Publishers
6300 Main
Kansas City, Missouri 64113

Phone: (816) 822-8295
E-mail: timedoc@compuserve.com
Fax: (816) 822-8295